Becoming Europeans?

Becoming Europeans?

Attitudes, Behaviour, and Socialization in the European Parliament

Roger Scully

Department of International Politics
University of Wales, Aberystwyth

OXFORD
UNIVERSITY PRESS

OXFORD

UNIVERSITY PRESS

Great Clarendon Street, Oxford OX2 6DP

Oxford University Press is a department of the University of Oxford.
It furthers the University's objective of excellence in research, scholarship,
and education by publishing worldwide in

Oxford New York

Auckland Cape Town Dar es Salaam Hong Kong Karachi
Kuala Lumpur Madrid Melbourne Mexico City Nairobi
New Delhi Shanghai Taipei Toronto

With offices in

Argentina Austria Brazil Chile Czech Republic France Greece
Guatemala Hungary Italy Japan Poland Portugal Singapore
South Korea Switzerland Thailand Turkey Ukraine Vietnam

Oxford is a registered trade mark of Oxford University Press
in the UK and in certain other countries

Published in the United States
by Oxford University Press Inc., New York

British Library Cataloguing in Publication Data
Data available

Library of Congress Cataloguing in Publication Data
Data available

Typeset by SPI Publisher Services, Pondicherry, India
Printed in Great Britain
on acid-free paper by
Biddles Ltd, King's Lynn, Norfolk

ISBN 0-19-928432-6   978-0-19-928432-0

1 3 5 7 9 10 8 6 4 2

Preface and Acknowledgements

Nationalism has been and remains the most important political phenomenon of the last three centuries. For good and ill, nationalism has come to dominate the manner in which most of our world is politically organized, and it remains overwhelmingly the main legitimizing principle of states (and would-be states). The European Union (EU) is the most far-reaching attempt to address the biggest problems that nationalism generates. At one and the same time, the EU upholds the centrality of nation-states within Europe, yet also partially subverts that dominance by establishing and developing important institutions of governance at a level beyond the state. There can be few, if any, more compelling scholarly tasks than trying to understand the process of European integration and its consequences.

I have been studying the EU for some years. Being a part of the research community engaged in this task has often been an exciting intellectual experience. Recent years have seen great developments in our subject matter as the EU has experienced both the 'deepening' of integration and the 'widening' of its membership to a degree that would have been difficult to imagine even twenty years ago. And, partly in response to these external stimuli, there has been a considerable degree of intellectual development among the scholarly community. Those studying the EU have raised their game substantially, with increasingly sophisticated concepts, theories and methods being deployed in their analysis. The *sui generis* and rapidly changing nature of the EU places immense demands on those attempting to understand it. It is not, I think, unduly complacent to suggest that scholars have become increasingly competent in fulfilling this very difficult task.

And yet there remain areas where thinking has lagged behind, and where one can still see in much (often otherwise highly sophisticated) academic work on the EU, pervasive assumptions that lack any clear theoretical grounding or empirical foundation. When such problematic assumptions have come to impinge in important ways on central intellectual questions for students of the EU—such as how we understand the integration process to proceed, and how we understand the nature of politics that operates in the institutions of the EU—then the critical assessment of these assumptions is important and long overdue.

Such is the starting point for this book. The idea that political actors in European institutions are subject to a strong tendency to 'go native' (as it is sometimes simplistically put) is not necessarily implausible. However, the adequacy of this assumption about socialization effects within EU institutions has never been properly investigated. It cannot be satisfactory that much academic literature simply *assumes* this to occur, without having established clearly either: (i) that this actually does happen; or (ii) *why* it should occur. A serious study of whether political actors in the EU do tend to 'go native' or not—and if so, why; if not, why not—is long overdue. Of course, this ground is covered to a significant extent in Liesbet Hooghe's excellent study of the European Commission (EC) (*The European Commission and the Integration of Europe: Images of Governance*, Cambridge University Press, 2001). However, Hooghe's book is essentially a study of the political preferences of EC officials which, as such, touches in several places on socialization as one possible explanation of those preferences, but does not amount to a sustained investigation of socialization per se. This means that (notwithstanding the many other contributions her book makes) it is not able to draw the broader conclusions about the importance of socialization for understanding EU institutions and European integration that this study attempts to do.

Drawing on several independent sources of data, I show that, within the European Parliament (EP) at least, a 'going native' hypothesis is simply not empirically supported by the evidence.

And I ground the presentation of this empirical evidence in a discussion that explains why such a finding should not really surprise us. Ultimately, this has some important implications for how we think about the EP and its members. But even more fundamentally, it matters for how scholars understand the process of European integration to proceed, and for how we think about processes of institutional socialization more generally, even outside the EU.

Writing this book was only possible with help from many people. First and foremost are those who are the subject matter of the study—Members of the EP. I thank those whom I interviewed in researching this book and my other work on the EP; almost without exception they were courteous and extremely helpful. I also thank the many staff in the EP who provided assistance along the way.

For encouraging me—often without realizing it—to develop the ideas in this book, I thank many present and former colleagues and students at Ohio State, Brunel, and Aberystwyth. And I must particularly thank Charlotte Burns, Neil Carter, David Farrell, Tapio Raunio, and Richard Wyn Jones for reading most or all of the manuscript and making many helpful suggestions. Simon Hix not only read much of the text, but also provided some of the data analysed in Chapters 4 and 5; I thank him for this, and also for intellectual stimulation over the years.

The greatest thanks, however, must be reserved for my family: to Marian, and to my parents, Rodney and Margaret. I am pleased to be able to dedicate this book, though quite inadequate repayment for their unfailing love and support, to them.

Roger Scully

Contents

I

Introduction

Perhaps the most frequent statement in contemporary political science is that 'institutions matter'. In recent times a variety of 'new institutionalisms' have emerged and achieved intellectual prominence—often differing widely in the arguments they develop, and even the definition of 'institutions' they deploy, but sharing the central tenet that an appreciation of the institutional context is essential for understanding politics, and the behaviour of political actors. Assorted institutions have been demonstrated to have fundamental and lasting effects: through shaping the political choices open to actors; by incorporating certain political preferences and values into the 'core' structures of a political system; and in influencing long-term patterns of political development.[1]

Nowhere has the renaissance of institutional political science been more pertinent than in the study of the European Union (EU)—not least because, nowhere are political institutions of more clear and fundamental importance. The EU is distinctive, above all, because it represents a uniquely institutionalized form of international cooperation. The creed of Jean Monnet, perhaps the key 'founding father' of European integration, was that 'nothing is possible without men [sic]; nothing is lasting without institutions'.[2] Though rarely developing in line with the precise path

[1] Examples of these different strands of 'new institutionalist' research are legion: for probably the best contemporary overview, see Peters (1999). For an overview of institutionalist research in the context of the EU, see Aspinwall and Schneider (2000).

[2] Quoted in Dinan (1999: 14).

advocated by Monnet, the EU has come to possess probably the most developed set of institutions (using that term in both of its common senses, to refer both to organizational entities, and to formal or informal rules) ever created through interstate co-operation. That such structures could be built on a legacy of centuries of fratricidal division in Europe is perhaps the most extraordinary aspect of the remarkable political achievement that the EU constitutes.

It is, thus, unsurprising that considerable research into the functioning and consequences of EU institutions is pursued, and that this work is central to contemporary study of the EU. Many of the key scholarly debates of recent years have been focused around institutional questions. One long-running dispute concerns whether and how some of the central institutional entities in the EU, and particularly the European Commission (EC), have exercised an independent and significant influence over the development of European integration.[3] A second important body of work emerging in recent years has explored how the different institutional procedures that exist for the passage of European legislation may shape politics and policymaking within the EU.[4] In common with institutionalist perspectives elsewhere in political science, contributors to these, and other debates about the EU have essentially been concerned with two issues: first, actors' preferences over, and attempts to shape, institutional arrangements; and second, the impact of institutions, once in place, on actors' behaviour.

Much of this institutionally centred work in EU studies follows the commonplace assumption that 'preferences' (political actors' desired states of affairs and their degree of favourability regarding alternative choices) are exogenously determined and can be

---

[3] For recent manifestations of this dispute, see Stone Sweet and Sandholtz (1998, 1999) who are essentially supportive of the idea that institutions such as the EC have exerted an important influence on the development of integration, and Moravcsik (1998, 1999) who takes a broadly contrary position.

[4] For examples of this debate, see Garrett and Tsebelis (1996, 2000), Tsebelis and Garrett (1997), Moser (1996), Scully (1997a) and Rittberger (2000).

treated as stable. What then becomes of analytical interest is how such preferences are pursued and with what consequences. But a substantial amount of other work on the EU takes a more far-reaching and radical perspective in suggesting, at least implicitly, that an assumption of stable preferences may be particularly problematic when applied to those working within the principal institutions of European cooperation. Experience within bodies like the EC, European Court of Justice (ECJ) and European Parliament (EP), it has frequently been argued, promotes a transformation in political attitudes and alters individuals' perceptions of their core interests and values.

These arguments have a long-standing and wide currency, but diverse origins. For some, they have been integral to the explanation of European integration, and grounded in the belief that the integration process is about far more than simply, cooperation between countries. An early statement of this perspective was that famously articulated by Haas (1968: 16) in his pioneering study of the early years of the EU,

Political integration is the process whereby political actors in several distinct national settings are persuaded to shift their *loyalties*, expectations and political activities towards a new centre.   (Emphasis added)

For Haas, the vanguard of the process of integration would be political elites working in new European institutions, amongst whom the transformation of loyalties might be most intense. Subsequent to Haas's work, similar notions concerning the impact of a process of socialization into 'Europeanism' on individuals have continued to pervade a substantial variety of writing about the EU. Such ideas make frequent appearances in textbooks, and continue to be important to the research output of some schools of thought which suggest that participation in the institutions and practices of the EU alters not only the identities and preferences of states (e.g. Stone Sweet and Sandholtz 1997; Sandholtz and Stone Sweet 1998) but also those of individual political actors directly engaged in the process (Armstrong and Bulmer 1998; Lewis 1998). To give one important example, recent work that builds on the insights of the broader 'social constructivist' intellectual school, and seeks to apply them to the study of the EU, has argued:

European integration has a transformative impact on the European state system and its constituent units... it is reasonable to assume that in the process agents' identity and subsequently their interests have equally changed. (Christiansen et al. 1999: 529; see also Wind 1997; Checkel 2001*a*, *b*, 2003)

But the idea that EU institutions exert a strong socializing impact on those serving within them extends well beyond academic writing. Similar notions pervade journalistic observation and statement about the EU. In the latter realm, there have frequently been claims, albeit sometimes expressed in a crude and even pejorative fashion, that those involved in EU politics are highly likely to 'go native'—becoming, over time, progressively more integrationist in their views, and 'European' in their values and outlook.[5]

The idea that experience in European institutions might transform preferences among political actors is not, however, merely a widely held one. It is also both intellectually plausible, and highly important. It is plausible because (as is discussed in Chapter 3), this notion is broadly consistent with perspectives from various academic disciplines, including some highly influential strains of current social and political theory, that attest to the transformative, socializing power of institutional settings.

The importance of such arguments lies in their implications of how we understand and study the EU. First and foremost, they have major implications for the process of European integration. If socialization into 'Europeanism' is as ubiquitous as is sometimes suggested then, as Haas first recognized, the development of increasingly like-minded actors in the central institutions of the EU provides at least a partial explanation for the advancement of integration. On the other hand, if such socialization arguments

---

[5] Although the terminology of 'going native' is generally pejorative, it is also used in places by academics analysing the possibility of institutional socialization in contexts like that of the EU—see, for example, Checkel (2003).

are not supported by the evidence of detailed empirical investigations, then an important element of some theoretical accounts is weakened; scholars may then be required to look to other processes and actors in order to explain satisfactorily the advance of European unity.

A second important implication concerns how scholars understand and study specific EU institutions—an area of growing intellectual attention. 'Going native'-type arguments depend upon, but also substantially reinforce, a particular view of EU bodies. That is, they imply environments that are sufficiently separated from the concerns and practices of national politics as to generate distinct and widely shared common values into which new members can become inculcated. Empirical support for the idea that EU institutions tend to socialize their members into greater 'Europeanism' would strengthen substantially the broader understanding of such bodies upon which this specific idea is based. On the other hand, falsification of this hypothesis would likely necessitate quite a different view of the EC, ECJ, and/or EP.

In short, the notion that those serving within EU institutions are subject to a pervasive socialization process, tending to promote an enhanced sense of 'Europeanism' that encompasses greater support for integration, is widespread, plausible and distinctly non-trivial. One might therefore expect this to be an area of intense scholarly activity. The reality, as Peterson (1997:11) has correctly observed, is that, '[r]elatively little research has been done on the way in which actors in Brussels are socialized to "Europeanism" '. Hypotheses have rarely been clearly specified or systematically investigated, and the limited empirical work that has been conducted generally suffers from insufficiencies of data and/or inadequate research designs (Pollack 1998). All too often these empirical weaknesses have been compounded by fundamental theoretical problems, with analyses remaining strikingly vague both on the precise changes posited to occur, and the nature of the political experience prompting these supposed shifts.

This situation is both astonishing and rather damning for the field of EU studies. It also has serious intellectual consequences. As long as this situation persists, an important dimension of integration theory, and a central feature of our understanding of EU institutions, must remain grounded in supposition rather than in the support of clear theorizing and strong empirical evidence. This is surely an unacceptable state of affairs for any field of study aspiring to be a serious intellectual enterprise.

This book responds to the current situation by conducting a detailed examination of the extent to which socialization processes shape the attitudes and behaviours of members of an increasingly important institution within the EU, namely the EP. The study has three specific goals. The first is to address the *theoretical* inadequacies of previous work. Drawing on the best of the existing body of work, can we develop a coherent articulation of why, how, and when political actors within EU institutions might be expected to 'go native'? And can we give a coherent articulation of reasons why (or the circumstances under which) such actors might remain relatively impervious to such pressures? The study offers answers to these questions.

The second goal of the study is to make a major *empirical* advance on previous work. Within the context of the EP, can we identify and analyse evidence in a manner that tells us whether and how, the attitudes and behaviours of a set of political actors alters after experience in a major EU institution? In order to address this question, several sources of original data on EP members' attitudes and behaviours are analysed.

The final goal of the book is to develop the broader implications of the study. What do the specific findings of the study tell us generally about socialization as a motor of European integration, and about the politics of institutions like Europe's elected parliament? And can it tell us anything about institutional socialization processes in general?

The remainder of this introductory chapter is devoted to three tasks. First, I provide a brief introduction to the chosen research site for the study, the EP. This introduction explains why the Parliament provides a highly appropriate focus for examining the general issue that is addressed by the book. Next, I briefly discuss some of the methodological issues raised by the study, and how they are dealt with. Finally, I elaborate on how subsequent chapters develop the main arguments.

Politics in the European Parliament

As of 1 May 2004, with the expansion of the EU's membership, the EP is an elected institution with 732 members (MEPs) from 25 EU member states and substantial powers in many areas. The origins of the chamber were very different. The institution was first established in 1952 as the Common Assembly of the European Coal and Steel Community (ECSC), the initial incarnation of the EU. At this stage, the assembly was of marginal importance. While substantive powers of decision within the new Community were given to the Council of Ministers (direct representatives of the governments of each member state) and the High Authority (later the EC, the quasi-executive body at the heart of the Community), the Assembly was established essentially to inject a modicum of parliamentary oversight into this new system. Its membership originally comprised a small number of members from each of the national parliaments of Community member states and it was granted few practical powers.

Much has changed, however, since these early days. The EP (as it renamed itself in 1962) became a directly elected institution in 1979. Though the five-yearly elections to the parliament have been justifiably criticized on many grounds—notably, for failing to generate public debate on European issues, and in practice often appearing little more than a series of 'super opinion polls' on national governments in each member state—the position of being the only directly elected EU body has provided the Parliament with at least a veneer of democratic credibility. This apparent status as 'voice of the people' in EU affairs has been exploited by many MEPs to argue the case for their being granted greater prerogatives, as a means of combating the much-touted 'democratic deficit' in the EU. Gradually, though in some cases reluctantly, national governments have used treaty amendments to enhance the powers of the Parliament. This occurred first in the realm of the EU budget, in the 1970s; and more recently, in several stages, for parliamentary powers over European legislation. The EP has also been given a greater role in the appointment of the EC. In short, the EP is now a political arena of substantial importance within the institutional structures of the EU.

As the EP's position within the institutional structures of the EU has altered, it has also—and to a substantial degree in response to these broader changes—experienced considerable internal institutional development (Kreppel 2002). The chamber has continued to refine its powerful committee system; the overwhelming proportion of parliamentarians are now effectively full-time MEPs, as the number of 'dual mandate' representatives (i.e. those who are simultaneously members of a national or regional chamber) has diminished (Corbett et al. 2000: 50); and the high levels of absenteeism for which the Parliament was, in its early years as an elected body, justifiably criticized, have been significantly reduced. Broadly speaking, as the EP has gained and used more serious powers, it has started to look and act like a more serious institution. And, in turn, more serious attention has been paid to the EP by outsiders—to some extent by journalists, and to a greater degree by both political lobbyists and scholars.

The growing powers and influence of the EP (which are outlined in greater detail in Chapter 2) provide a small part of the reasoning for focusing this study upon the chamber: quite simply, as the Parliament has grown in importance, so has scholars' need for knowledge about it. Of far greater importance, however, is that we have very strong prima facie grounds for regarding the EP as a particularly appropriate context in which to examine the key issue at stake in this book—socialization processes in EU institutions. A principal reason for this is that parliamentary bodies have often been identified as being highly effective in socializing their new members. As Marquand observes (1979: 75):

Parliaments are even better at indoctrinating their members with their own norms than are public schools or miners' lodges, as a whole list of angry firebrands who later mellowed into sage and gradualist parliamentary statesmen bears witness.[6]

Specific work on the EP has often taken a similar line (see Chapter 3): the consistently pro-integrationist line taken by the chamber has been attributed, at least in part, to members becoming socialized into more pro-European attitudes by their experiences in the Parliament. We would seem to have good cause to regard the EP as an institutional context in which the socialization effects attributed more generally to European institutions can be expected to work with particular power.

An additional and somewhat more pragmatic reason for considering the EP as an appropriate research site is that, in comparison to other EU institutions, the Parliament offers greater scope for gaining empirical leverage on our research question. Quite simply, measures of attitudes and behaviours on European integration can be more readily generated from the membership of the EP, than from those working in other EU bodies. This is a more than trivial consideration. As discussed in the following section of this chapter, there are considerable difficulties inherent in measuring the impact (or lack thereof) of socialization processes; these difficulties help to account for many of the empirical weaknesses in the existing body of work in this area. The fact that we possess, for relatively large numbers of MEPs, both detailed survey data about their political attitudes and publicly available information about important aspects of their political behaviour, offers substantial potential for rigorous empirical analysis.

A note on methodology

To what extent an individual MEP is socialized into a Euro-mindedness or has become an MEP because he or she adhered to such beliefs in the first place *must* remain a matter of argument   (Johanssen 1995: 23, emphasis added).

---

[6] For classic discussions of parliaments as socializing institutions, see Asher (1973), Fenno (1962, 1973), and Searing (1986).

Johanssen is wrong. It is possible to conduct serious empirical research into the question this study addresses. Doing so, however, is difficult; for the study to be accomplished with any degree of success requires that serious attention be paid to some important issues of method.

At least three issues require attention. The first concerns the dependent variable of our analysis. To assess whether MEPs do tend to 'go native' over time, we need a reasonably clear idea of what would be the observable implications of such a process. In line with the discussion above, this is interpreted here as meaning attitudes and behaviours of MEPs that appear to be clearly 'pro-integration'. However, given that scholars of the EU have found it far from straightforward to come up with a clear definition of what European integration is,[7] measuring attitudes and behaviours in relation to this concept is not likely to be very easy.

Two further methodological issues that must be addressed are both captured well in the following quote from Mughan et al. (1997: 94–5). Talking in the specific context of their study of deradicalization amongst British Labour MPs, they observe:

The socialization of professional politicians is . . . not readily visible at any single point in time . . . legislators may not themselves be aware of their attitudinal conservatization. Behavioural anomalies can always be rationalized away by 'the circumstances', and need not be admitted to reflect more profound changes in ways of thinking . . . even if legislators admit to themselves that their radical instincts have waned, they will commonly deny it, for any number of good reasons—loss of self-respect for 'selling out', concern about not being renominated by more radical constituency parties, fear of electoral reprisal and so on.

The first issue raised here concerns what are reliable data sources with which to measure attitudes and behaviours. The second issue is how one can best measure a potentially moving target,

---

[7] For instance, Ernst Haas observed in 1971, after many years of work in the area, that '[a] giant step on the road toward an integrated theory of regional integration . . . would be taken if we could clarify the matter of what we propose to explain'(Haas 1971: 26; see also Rosamond 2000: 9–14).

that is whether or not attitudes and behaviours are changing over time.

One approach that has been taken to dealing with all three methodological issues is the use of in-depth interviews with a substantial sample of members of one or more EU institutions. These interviews can then be used to probe those concerned and ask them directly about their perceptions of attitudinal and/or behavioural changes: do they believe that they have been socialized into becoming more pro-integration?[8] The in-depth interview has many strengths as a research method for social scientists, and material from such interviews conducted with MEPs will indeed be used as an important source of information in this study, particularly in Chapter 2. Only the most arrogant of social scientists could dismiss the importance of allowing those whom we study to give their views on the matter in question, in the terminology that appears most appropriate to them. And yet, even though this is fully acknowledged, it is clear that there are also serious methodological problems with using interviews as the main source of evidence for the study of socialization effects. First, as suggested above, interview responses are subject to contamination by 'socially desirable' responses. Second, interviews do not provide any *independent* validation of whether socialization effects that are perceived on the part of the interviewee actually do influence broader political attitudes and behaviours. And third, as is discussed in further detail in Chapter 2, interview questions about socialization effects place very heavy, and almost certainly quite unreasonable, interpretative burdens on interviewees. It should be clear, then, that an interview-based research strategy cannot provide a sound evidential basis for the empirical investigation of institutional socialization effects. Thus, the bulk of the empirical research conducted in this study draws on other sources of evidence and methods of analysis.

First, to address the problem of how to specify the dependent variable, we deploy several alternative measures of MEPs' relevant

---

[8] This is, indeed, broadly the approach taken by several scholars—see Chapter 3.

attitudes and behaviours. While this strategy does raise the potential problem of explaining conflicting findings derived from different measures, it has the compensating strength that if the empirical findings are broadly consistent, they cannot then be criticized as being an artefact on one particular, and conceivably inappropriate, measure. The approach taken thus follows Putnam's highly apposite advice (1993: 12; see also King et al. 1994):

> The prudent social scientist, like the wise investor, must rely on diversification to magnify the strengths, and to offset the weaknesses, of any single instrument.

Specifically, we draw on representative survey data of MEPs' political attitudes, and behavioural data drawn from votes in the EP. These data do not suffer from the problem of interviewee rationalization pointed to above, and thus resolve our second methodological problem. However, there remains the issue of how these data can be used to inform us about the presence or absence of attitudinal and behavioural changes over time on the part of MEPs. The ideal situation would be where one possessed time-series data—where the same factor was measured for a number of individuals at several different points in time. Where, as in this study, such time-series are mostly unavailable, investigators are forced to fall back on cross-sectional data (i.e. measurements at a single point in time) that, for the purposes of a study like this one, have some important limitations. Specifically, such data cannot directly identify change over time (or its absence), but can only point to observable implications that are *consistent with* change (or the absence of it). Thus, for instance, Mughan et al. attempt to 'map' the growing institutional conservatism of previously radical politicians—but are unable, using the cross-sectional data of behaviour in particular parliamentary votes actually to show any individual-level change, although their findings are certainly consistent with such change.[9] This does not mean that we should

---

[9] In a very similar way to the work of Mughan et al. (1997), much of the literature on mass political socialization uses cross sectional data to examine posited changes

dismiss such work; merely that, as with much political enquiry, we have to acknowledge that imperfect data allow us only partial insight into the matters with which we are concerned.

A specific concern of testing for a dynamic effect (socialization over time) with cross-sectional data, is highlighted in an interesting discussion on institutional socialization in the EP by Shepherd (1996). He observes that it may often be difficult empirically to disentangle an institutional loyalty that derives from a long-term 'careerist' commitment to service in an institution (which may be present from the beginning of a legislative career) from that which has been acquired over time via a socialization process. If significant socialization processes are present, then one should expect to see a positive relationship between length of service and members' institutional loyalty. If, on the other hand, purely careerist considerations were at work, one would still expect to see essentially the same statistical relationship. This is because while both careerists and non-careerists should be present in the less experienced cohorts, only careerists—following Scarrow's definition (1997: 262) of a 'European career' MEP as being a member who 'served for at least eight years . . . without winning a new national legislative seat or holding a dual mandate for more than two years'—will be present in significant numbers among more experienced members. However, while a fine distinction between careerism and socialization may not be possible from such a test, one can have a fair degree of confidence that neither process is present if no significant statistical relationship exists. Thus, for the purposes of this study what is important is whether large numbers of MEPs endorse a pro-integrationist position, and when in their career as a member they do so.

The survey data deployed here comprise two major surveys of parliamentarians, conducted in 1996 and 2000. The former survey interviewed members of national parliaments alongside members of the EP, the latter focused on MEPs alone. Particularly relevant

---

over time in political attitudes—for a classic example, see Converse (1969; although also see Abramson 1992 for an important methodological critique).

to this study are questions concerning parliamentarians' sense of identity, their attitudes towards European integration in general, and their views on important policy issues and on the role of the EP within the EU in particular. An institutional socialization hypothesis would suggest a positive correlation between service (and also length of service) in the EP on the one hand, and greater European identity, favourability to integration and to enhanced European policy competences and a greater role for the Parliament on the other. As the data analysed only incorporate one 'wave' surveys—as opposed to 'panel data', wherein the same respondents are re-interviewed once or more—we are thus inherently limited in our ability to analyse change over time. However, by controlling for a number of other pertinent factors that might shape attitudes, and by developing several different comparisons between MEPs and their national counterparts, and within the sample of MEPs alone, the validity of the analysis can be substantially strengthened.

In addition, however, we also analyse MEPs' behaviour on several important votes held in the EP over recent years. All the votes examined took place in the context of intergovernmental conferences (IGCs) within the EU that were considering, among other matters, various measures of institutional reform in the EU that could have the effect of deepening integration and enhancing the powers of the Parliament itself. Although marginalized in the decision-making process of the IGCs, the parliament nonetheless had a clear interest in the outcome of the conference, and unsurprisingly sought to make its opinions known. The resolutions debated and voted on in the EP thus brought to the fore MEPs' views on European unity, as well as those of their parties (both national and European); what was at stake was not simply an attitude, but the willingness of members to follow up such attitudes by taking a very public stand on important issues.

Once again, there are limits and potential problems to the use of such data. We are, once again, dealing here with essentially cross-sectional data. A further problem is that MEPs may be subject to a number of different considerations shaping how they vote, of which their own attitudes to the issue in questions will be only one. Other plausible influences may include pressure from colleagues or their national party: thus, an MEP may take a particular line not because they truly support it, but because to do otherwise would incur the displeasure of colleagues whose support is needed on other issues, or to help that MEP to win some measure of advance in their political career. Another limitation of the data is that at best, voting analysis can give us only limited insight into the intensity of individuals' views: with only a few voting options (the EP allows MEPs to vote in favour or against something, or to register an abstention, as well as not participating in the vote) we cannot know whether an individuals' endorsement means grudging support, modest enthusiasm or passionate conviction. Nonetheless, roll-call votes have become one of the most widely used forms of data used to analyse the attitudes and behaviours of parliamentarians (Mezey 1993: 342). And the reasons for this are not hard to deduce. Unlike information gathered by surveys or interviews, roll-call votes cannot be dismissed as mere 'cheap talk'. Instead they constitute 'hard' data based on real behaviour by politicians when important issues were being decided. By measuring across several important votes, and controlling for other salient influences on MEPs' behaviour, we can gain additional insight into whether the forces of institutional socialization tend to make them vote in a more clearly 'pro-European' manner in key parliamentary divisions.

Finally, and in response to the inherent limits of cross-sectional survey and voting data, a very different form of analysis of MEPs voting is deployed. Rather than examining their behaviour on specifically integration-related divisions, this looks at the behaviour of new MEPs over the first months of a parliamentary term. One manifestation of a greater 'Euro-mindedness' among MEPs might be for them to identify increasingly with their multi-national party group in the EP, and not to see themselves solely or mainly as members of a national party. The analysis therefore examines whether MEPs become increasingly likely, as they acclimatize to life in the EP, to defect from their national party group line on occasions when that line differs from the position of the majority in the broader party group.

Plan of the book

The rest of the book is developed over six chapters. Chapter 2 lays out the context of the study by providing a detailed introduction to the EP and its membership. The chapter first takes an 'external' view of the chamber, explaining how the EU's elected institution has grown substantially in importance relative to the other main bodies within the EU. (It is noted here that one common explanation for the Parliament's success in developing its role is the tendency of its membership to be socialized into commitment to this project.) The chapter then moves on to an 'internal' examination of the EP, explaining the main features of the Parliament's own organizational structures, and indicating how these help define the type of politics that occurs within the chamber. The third section of the chapter draws on in-depth interviews conducted with a large number of MEPs where politicians explained why they sought election to the Parliament, and gave their own perceptions of the prevalence of socialization effects within the EP. As will be seen, many of those interviewed believe that there is a tendency for MEPs to become more European-minded in various senses. However, the final section of the chapter explains why we cannot rest content with this evidence of MEPs' own perceptions. It argues that there is a need for further study both to consider the theoretical basis for any hypothesized socialization effects, and to examine other empirical evidence to assess whether such effects are actually manifested.

Chapter 3 takes the study forward by reviewing in detail the state of our existing knowledge about the subject matter of this study. In line with MEPs' perceptions, notions of pervasive socialization processes leading to attitudinal and behavioural changes for those serving within European institutions are shown to be widespread, appearing in much popular commentary and in a great deal of academic literature on the EU, including that on the EP. However, the discussion then goes on to demonstrate that strikingly little evidence has ever actually been presented to support the central hypothesis common to this literature: that significant socialization effects operating among members of EU institutions lead to changes in attitudes and/or behaviours in an identifiably more pro-European direction. Virtually all the empirical work in this area hitherto has produced indeterminate or null findings; furthermore, coherent theoretical foundations that might underpin the assumption of actors 'going native' in EU institutions have almost never been explicitly developed alongside the conduct of serious empirical research.[10]

Chapter 4 undertakes the task of developing a coherent explanation of the circumstances in which political actors operating within EU institutions might be subject to socialization processes that shape their attitudes and behaviours in a more integrationist direction. Any such coherent explanation, it is argued, must depend on two core elements: an understanding of the nature of the socializing experience to be undergone, and assumptions about the individuals who will undergo this experience. The chapter then goes on to discuss the likely implications of this framework for socialization processes in the EP. The discussion shows that the extent to which MEPs become divorced from the national political scene has been substantially overstated. And it is argued that a rationalist understanding of MEPs' core political goals— assumed to be policy, office and (re-)election—would predict that European Parliamentarians should prove relatively immune to any pressures to 'go native'.

Chapters 5 and 6 take the empirical analysis of the study further. Chapter 5 examines the potential impact of institutional socialization processes in the EP on the attitudes of MEPs. Survey data is used to examine parliamentarians' opinions on a variety of matters related to the development of European integration. A direct

---

[10] A important partial exception, discussed in Chapters 3 and 4, is the work of Checkel (2001, 2003).

comparison of MEPs with members of national parliaments shows no substantial relationship between service in the EP and more 'pro-European' views. And a more detailed assessment, concentrating solely on EP members, finds that those who have been in the Parliament for a greater length of time—and thus have had a greater exposure to the putative impact of institutional socialization—are no more likely to claim a 'European' identify, or to favour the deepening of integration or the extension of the powers of the EP, than their less experienced colleagues.

Chapter 6 switches attention away from measures of political attitudes to the consideration of MEPs' behaviour in the parliament. Multivariate analysis of MEPs' behaviour on several key votes in the chamber that were concerned directly with the advancement of European integration demonstrates there to be no consistent relationship between greater experience in the chamber (and thus longer exposure to the forces of socialization) and support for advancing European unity. And a time-series analysis of the behaviour of new MEPs during the first months of the 1999–2004 Parliament shows no tendency for them to become increasingly likely to side with their European rather than national party colleagues when these two forms of party loyalty come into conflict.

Chapter 7 concludes the study by summarizing the major findings presented, and dealing with some obvious potential objections to the conclusions drawn, before going on to assess their broader implications. In line with the rationalist perspective developed in Chapter 4, the overwhelming preponderance of evidence examined in this study shows little sign that service in the EP leads to its members 'going native'. Three broad implications of these empirical findings are then discussed. First, we consider what the study tells us about the EP as an institution. The EP, it is suggested, fits much less well than other EU entities into its traditional classification as a 'supranational' body; to a very considerable extent, MEPs remain nationally based politicians, albeit ones operating for significant periods of time in a European setting. Second, we assess the implications of the findings for other EU institutions and for European integration. The argument is made that the value changes anticipated by scholars from Haas onwards are far more conditional than has often been presumed. It is not simply being 'in Europe' that promotes attitudinal and behavioural changes in a more pro-integration direction; such changes are only likely to arise when they are consistent with the particular institutional settings that political actors find themselves in, and the relationship of those settings to the actors' core goals. We cannot assume that people will 'become Europeans' without examining the basis for any such changes in specific institutional contexts. Thus, socialization effects must play a much more limited role in explanations of European integration than many scholars have believed. Finally, the wider implications of this study for the analysis of institutional socialization as a general phenomenon are considered.

The Institutional Context—Europe's Elected Parliament

The aim of this chapter is to establish the context for the study by providing a detailed introduction to the EP. For reasons explained in Chapter 1, any conclusions drawn from the book should have a relevance that extends beyond this particular institution; nonetheless, these conclusions are only likely to carry conviction in the first place if the study is clearly grounded in an informed understanding of the EP. The first two sections of the chapter therefore outline, respectively, the place of the EP within the broader institutional structures of the EU, and the main features of the internal organization of the Parliament. An extended discussion of these two aspects is important, both because each has seen considerable change over recent times, and also because—as will be seen—they have important implications for the plausibility of a 'going native' hypothesis. The third section of the chapter draws on in-depth interviews conducted with MEPs themselves. This section establishes that while the idea of service in the EP exerting some socialization effects is accepted by most MEPs, and many even assent to the idea that they may tend to become more pro-integration over time, there is limited consensus among them about either the precise form of such change or the processes that prompt it to occur. This then provides the basis for the argument in the concluding section of the chapter, which explains why interview data on MEPs' perceptions cannot by itself provide a sound empirical basis for the investigation of institutional socialization processes in the EP, and why a detailed study of this phenomenon is required.

From insipid assembly to powerful Parliament[1]

The June 2004 elections to the EP witnessed those lucky enough to be elected as MEPs receive popular mandates to serve in an institution that could exert substantial powers in many areas. They could thus look forward to political life in a very different sort of institution than the one their first predecessors had served in, more than fifty years ago. This section explains some of the major changes that have occurred in the status of the EP.

What is now the EP began life as the Common Assembly of the nascent ECSC in 1952. The assembly was not central to the plans of the 'founding fathers' of integration. 'In Jean Monnet's vision, it was, together with the European Court of Justice[ECJ], an institution of control and scrutiny, not of decision-making' (Neunreither 2000: 133). Thus, the new chamber was given limited and specific powers. In the area of lawmaking it was very restricted: it could give only opinions (of a non-binding nature) on new policies and laws. It could, in principle, dismiss the High Authority (the forerunner to today's European Commission) for gross mismanagement. But other than that, it was restricted to discussion and scrutiny. Furthermore, the assembly's membership was not to be elected by voters; rather, the membership was drawn from among the members of member states' national parliaments. Though this provided a direct link between the ECSC and national political systems, it also ensured that the Common Assembly, as well as having restricted powers, could only ever be a part-time institution, as members still had national parliamentary responsibilities to fulfil.

The original, nominated, Common Assembly consisted of seventy-eight members from the then 6 ECSC member states. By May 2004, with the enlargement of the EU to twenty-five member

---

[1] This section draws heavily on the discussion in Scully (2003).

states, the EP (as it had renamed itself in 1962) comprised 732 elected representatives from the now twenty-five states inside the EU. (see Table 2.1 for a description of how the EP has enlarged over time.) The Rome Treaty in the late 1950s had called for the chamber to become an elected institution. However, the first EP elections did not take place until 1979. A central reason for this delay was that governments and parties, cautious about the development of stronger European-level institutions, foresaw that an elected EP would be in a powerful position to argue for greater powers: after all, the EP would be (as, indeed, it remains), the only directly elected European institution, and it could use this democratic legitimacy to argue for enhanced prerogatives for itself. Such fears proved wellfounded, and while substantial concerns persist regarding the extent to which EP elections actually function as an effective means by which the 'voice of the people' can

TABLE 2.1   The growth over time of the EP

Year	No. of MEPs	No. of member states	Status of MEPs	Title of chamber
1952	78	6	Nominated	ECSC Common Assembly
1958	142	6	Nominated	EC Common Assembly
1973	198	9[a]	Nominated	European Parliament
1979	410	9	Elected	European Parliament
1981	434	10[b]	Elected	European Parliament
1986	518	12[c]	Elected	European Parliament
1994	567	12[d]	Elected	European Parliament
1995	626	15[e]	Elected	European Parliament
2004	732	25[f]	Elected	European Parliament

[a]Enlargement to Denmark, Ireland, and UK
[b]Enlargement to Greece
[c]Enlargement to Portugal and Spain
[d]German enlargement and seat redistribution
[e]Enlargement to Austria, Finland, and Sweden
[f]Enlargement to Cyprus, Czech Republic, Estonia, Hungary, Latvia, Lithuania, Malta, Poland, Slovakia, and Slovenia

shape the EU (van der Eijk and Franklin 1996), the elected Parliament has proven to be a strong advocate, both of closer European integration in general, and more powers for itself in particular (Corbett 1998, 1999). Moreover, such pressure has been effective. By the mid-1990s, the EP was no longer a marginal institution, essentially shouting from the sidelines; rather, it was a central, 'mainstream' part of the EU's governing system.

Since the 1970s treaty amendments and institutional agreements have granted the EP considerably greater formal powers. (See Table 2.2 for a summary of the major changes described below.) The first major advance for the Parliament came in the realm of the community budget. Two treaties in the 1970s granted the Parliament the right to propose modifications to planned 'compulsory' spending (mainly on agriculture), to insist on amendments to 'non-compulsory' spending, and the right (if supported by an absolute majority of all MEPs, and two-thirds of

TABLE 2.2   The development of the EP powers

Year	Event	Impact on EP Powers
1970	Treaty changes on budget	Greater budgetary powers for EP
1975	Treaty changes on budget	More budgetary powers for EP; EP given considerable influence over non-CAP spending
1980	Isoglucose judgment of ECJ	Right of consultation for EP reinforced
1987	Entry into force of Single Act	Cooperation procedure introduced for some legislation, giving EP greater scope for delay, amendment and blocking laws; Assent powers to EP on some matters
1993	Maastricht Treaty enters into force	Co-decision procedure introduced for some legislation; EP given approval power over nominated Commission
1999	Amsterdam Treaty enters into force	Co-decision procedure altered in EP's favour, and extended in scope; EP given formal right to veto Commission President-nominee

those voting) to reject the budget outright.[2] The parliament's budgetary role was further enhanced from the late 1980s, by a series of 'Inter-institutional Agreements' between the Council, Commission, and Parliament, which agreed that parliamentary approval would henceforth be needed for increases in compulsory spending; these agreements ran parallel to multi-year budgetary deals that, by fixing for several years ahead, broad spending priorities, allowed the parliament to give greater attention to monitoring EU expenditure.

The Parliament has made more limited progress in terms of 'executive oversight', if only because the EU lacks a clear and distinct 'executive branch' of government to oversee. A substantial number of executive functions—particularly in foreign affairs—are wielded by national governments, who are reluctant to yield to EP scrutiny. Nonetheless, day-to-day scrutiny of the EC is increasingly pursued by EP committees. And the Parliament can still dismiss the EC, and in March 1999, would have used the power in response to evidence of mismanagement in the EC had they not been pre-empted by the resignation of all twenty Commissioners. And the EP's role was enhanced by the Maastricht Treaty, which gave the chamber approval power over the new EC nominated by national governments. This provision was interpreted in 1994–5 as allowing the Parliament both to vote on the Commission President-designate and on the EC as a whole; the Amsterdam Treaty formally approved the Parliament's veto over the President-designate. In the autumn of 2004, the credible threat of a parliamentary veto forced several changes to the new Barroso Commission.

---

[2] This power has been exercised twice—in 1979 and 1984. In the event of a rejection of the budget, the treaties allow the Community, however, to continue to exist for each month of the following year on the basis of 'twelfths': that is spending continues at a level equivalent to one-twelfth of appropriations for the previous financial year. 'Compulsory' spending is that which is a binding commitment arising out of EU treaties or legislation; 'non-compulsory' spending is all other EU spending. Each account for roughly 50 per cent of the EU budget.

The greatest and most recent advances by the EP are in the area of EU law making. Before the Single European Act, the EP's role here was very limited. EU laws (other than Commission legislation)[3] were processed via 'consultation'. The Parliament could offer an opinion, but could not force the EC or Council to respond to this opinion. Aside from using delaying tactics (by failing to present its opinion),[4] the EP had no formal mechanism of influencing legislation.

A fierce lobby for greater parliamentary powers bore some fruit in the Single Act. Consultation was retained for most laws. However, for most legislation related to the 'single market', the 'cooperation' procedure was introduced. This permitted the EP to propose amendments (which, if supported by the Commission, could be overturned only by a unanimous Council but accepted by a qualified majority of states), or issue a veto that could only be overturned by a unanimous Council of Ministers. This was undoubtedly a significant advance for the EP. The Single Act also gave the EP 'assent' power (i.e. a simple yes/no vote) over matters like association agreements with non-EU states, and the accession of new members to the EU.

The Maastricht Treaty produced a further significant change; after Maastricht, around one-quarter of laws were processed under another new procedure, 'co-decision'. Co-decision laws were designated as joint Acts of the Parliament and Council (rather than the Council alone), and the procedure added an irrevocable par-

---

[3] While virtually all major EU laws require endorsement by the Council of Ministers, the EC also has the ability to issues laws by itself. While the vast majority of these are very narrow and technical items, in terms of sheer quantity they nonetheless form the bulk of EU legislation (Nugent 1999: 123–4).

[4] The 1980 *Isoglucose* ruling of the Court of Justice did require that the EP be properly consulted over draft laws, generally interpreted to mean that the EP could delay matters by failing to offer its opinion, possibly indefinitely. Corbett et al. document the Commission changing a proposal (on the issue of economic and monetary union) in the face of a threatened Parliamentary delay (1995: 193). However, a judgement of the ECJ has stated that indefinite delay is not a legitimate Parliamentary tactic on legislation designated as 'urgent' by the Council (Corbett 1996: 39–40).

liamentary veto to previous arrangements. Most observers saw this as a considerable step forward:

Maastricht marks the point in the Community's development at which the Parliament became the first chamber of a real legislature.... The co-decision procedure means that it has now come of age as a lawmaking body   (Duff, 1994: 31).[5]

The 1997 Amsterdam Treaty revised co-decision in a manner some-what beneficial to the Parliament, and also extended it to further areas of EU law. The procedure is now used for around half of EU laws, with the vast majority of the rest operating under consultation.

The precise degree to which the various changes have boosted the EP's role within the institutional structures of the EU, and why, has been a matter of some scholarly debate. The formal powers granted to an institution only become relevant if there is at least some potential for those powers to be used. In the complex world of European lawmaking, where the EP has to interact with the Council and EC, some scholars argued that the veto power granted the EP under assent and co-decision would be of little benefit to the Parliament, as it would leave the EP with some uncomfortable 'take it or leave it' choices. A strong 'revisionist' perspective suggested that the cooperation procedure had actually given the EP greater scope to set the legislative agenda (see Garrett and Tsebelis 1996; Tsebelis and Garrett 1997). However, this argument, developed through abstract theoretical models of legislative bargaining, has been subject to theoretical criticism (Scully 1997a, 1997b; Moser 1997; Rittberger 2000) and has not

---

[5] It should be noted that the way in which Maastricht originally shaped the co-decision procedure did cause concern among many MEPs, because it appeared to allow for the Council, at the end of the procedure, to reject a compromise with Parliament and impose a 'take it-or leave it' choice on MEPs. This possibility not only prompted the academic debate referred to in the main text; it also led MEPs to revise their Rules of Procedure so as to make it as unlikely as possible that govern-ments would try to back MEPs into a corner. For further discussion of this, see Hix (2002b).

been supported by the empirical evidence: the Parliament's success in advancing legislative amendments increased significantly under co-decision compared to the cooperation procedure (Kreppel 1999; Shackleton 2000; Tsebelis et al. 2001).

As it entered the twenty-first century, the EP still had more restricted formal prerogatives than many national parliaments. But unlike most of the executive dominated national legislatures with which it might be compared, the EP has consistently shown a willingness to use many of its powers. In short, the EP is now a serious player in the institutional structures in the EU. This matters, of course, for the politics of the EU. By providing an additional 'veto-player' in the system (Tsebelis 2002), empowerment of the EP creates a policymaking process that almost certainly produces different outcomes than would otherwise be the case. But recognition of the empowerment of the EP also sharpens the focus of this study. The EP has received greater powers in part because it has consistently and effectively pressed for them (Rittberger 2003); it has been able to do this because the institution has consistently contained within it a majority of figures who are broadly pro-integration and have supported the development of the EP's prerogatives as a key element of the advancement of integration. One obvious explanation of the latter fact is that most MEPs are pro-integration because a process of socialization operating within the institutional environment of the EP acts to generate and reinforce such attitudes and behaviours. Testing whether this potentially plausible explanation is actually correct will be the task for much of this book.

Life inside the European Parliament

Joining the parliament is difficult, because they all seem to know so much, to understand its gibberish; even if you are listening to it in English you sometimes wonder... certainly it was at least six months before I felt I was starting to get a clue about what was going on. And I think it probably takes eighteen months to two years to get used to it, and you talk to some people who have been there for years and don't seem to know things. It's a very Byzantine type of organization (British MEP).[6]

One can well sympathize with the—not untypical—views of this politician. Life inside the EP is indeed complex. This complexity arises not only from the detailed and technical matters of EU policy that the Parliament spends much of its time dealing with; complexity is virtually inherent in the multinational, multilingual, and multiparty political environment that the EP constitutes. This section of the chapter highlights some of the major features of politics within the Parliament.

Amidst the complexity of life in the EP, much order can actually be discerned. At all levels, the Parliament has become a highly organized, highly 'institutionalized' chamber. This starts with the structuring of the EP's time. The Parliamentary timetable defines specific weeks as set aside for plenary sessions (usually one four-day session per month in Strasbourg, with a few additional 'mini sessions' of two days in Brussels); other weeks being for committee work (usually two weeks in a month); and the balance of time reserved for 'party group weeks' and 'constituency weeks'. This 'hyperorganization' of the parliamentary timetable extends into the conduct of plenary sessions. Largely because of the need for the provision of translation facilities, time for debates and individual contributions is rationed very precisely—literally almost down to the second.

Plenary sessions include the great set-piece occasions of the EP's business. MEPs are frequently addressed by Prime Ministers and Foreign Ministers of member states, and sometimes of third countries. And on occasion, as with the debates held in July 1994 and 1999 over the nominations of Jacques Santer and Romano Prodi respectively as Commission President, debates can be genuinely dramatic events. Far more commonly, plenary sessions are highly tedious: the problems of a multilingual institution hamper debate, and speeches tend to be more about putting certain views

[6] Interview, 23 July 1998.

'on the record' rather than trying to persuade anyone, while voting time witnesses large numbers of votes, often on unrelated topics, being held one after the other.

The Committees of the EP are widely regarded as the place where the bulk of the serious work of the EP is done. The EP now has a well-established system of permanent committees (seventeen in the 1999–2004 parliament). These committees cover most areas of EU policy, and individual committees undertake both legislative work (scrutinizing draft legislation and drawing up amendments) and oversight activity (looking into the conduct of policy) in their area of responsibility. Some committees have also taken on a broader role: the Institutional Affairs Committee in previous parliaments (now the Constitutional Affairs Committee) sought to develop visionary proposals for deepening integration; the Women's Rights and Equal Opportunities Committee has often sought to broaden the degree to which gender-related considerations are incorporated into the EU; and the Foreign Affairs Committee has rarely felt itself restricted to discuss matters strictly linked to the EU's Common Foreign and Security Policy. The work conducted by committees can sometimes be shaped by the influence of strong committee chairs. But, at least as often, committee work is shaped by the 'group coordinators' appointed by the major party groups to each committee (Whitaker 2001). And, on particular matters of policy, there is considerable scope for individual MEPs to have an impact, particularly if acting as *rapporteur*: the person delegated by a committee to prepare its report on a specific topic.

Probably the biggest single source of complexity in the daily life of the EP is the sheer diversity of nationalities, interests and political points of view represented there. MEPs in the 1999–2004 parliament represented over 100 separate national parties or similar organizations from the fifteen member states; with enlargement in 2004, the diversity of the chamber made a further, qualitative leap. Although turnover at each election tends to be high (in recent times about 50 per cent of members at the beginning of each parliament were not MEPs in the previous one; this percentage inevitably increased yet further with the 2004 enlargement), there are also a substantial number of representatives who have built long-term political careers at the European level.

MEPs from the different national parties join together in multinational party groups, based broadly around political ideology. The party groups themselves seek to bring together like-minded members from different states, yet they must always remain aware of the differing national traditions and interests within their ranks. Research conducted on the party groups has shown that in votes held in the EP the groups are—given the diversity of the membership of the larger ones in particular—quite remarkable for their high degree of unity: this is typically much higher than that displayed by the two parties in the US Congress, for instance (Raunio 1997; Hix and Lord 1997). Yet this unity must often be built on the basis of substantial 'give and take' between national delegations within the group, and often agreement is formed on the basis of the lowest common denominator; even so, dissent from party group positions most often occurs when large numbers of MEPs from one or more national delegation refuse to support a group line (Kreppel and Tsebelis 1999; Hix 2002a). (This issue is revisited in Chapter 6.)

Although the party groups are ideologically based, intergroup relations in the Parliament have traditionally been based on co-operation rather than confrontation. The largest groups in the chamber have always been from the centre-right (the European People's Party (EPP) group of Christian Democrats and some Conservatives) and the centre-left (the Party of European Socialists (PES) group representing moderate social democrats and socialists). For many years, these two blocs cooperated in sharing out most of the senior posts in the EP, as well as seeking consensus in most other matters before the Parliament.[7] The 1999–2004

---

[7] Among the posts open in the EP are President (Speaker) of the EP, a number of Vice-Presidents, and Committee and Delegation Chairships. The Conference of Presidents, which includes the EP President and Vice-Presidents, and the leaders (Presidents) of the Party Groups, is the main official forum in the EP for the

chamber saw increasing conflict between the major groups, however, and growing levels of voting division along left-right lines in the chamber (Hix 2002a). A prime example was the election of the EP's President: for some years, the two leading groups had shared this job (which is held by each incumbent for two and a half years, half of a five-year EP term) between them and supported each other's candidates when the other group's 'turn' came. In both July 1999 and January 2002, however, a PES candidate sought (unsuccessfully) the Presidency in opposition to candidates endorsed by the EPP.[8]

Compared to the executive-dominated parliaments of many countries in Europe, power in the EP is much more widely diffused. The lack of a controlling, 'governing' power in the chamber, the multiparty environment of the EP, and the fact that deployment of some of its major powers requires the mobilization of 'supermajorities',[9] makes compromise the order of the day, and places a premium on negotiating skills. However, as the chamber has gained powers, it has adjusted its internal ways of working to deal with its enhanced status as a more serious political institution. As the most detailed study of internal EP reform has observed,

[w]hen the EP was without direct legislative power and unable to effectively influence policy outcomes, the party groups had little need or desire to exert strict control over their membership. . . . However, as the EP acquired the power to impact legislative outcomes, the political groups

---

scheduling of parliamentary business, and the allocation of things like committee chairships.

[8] In 1999 the socialists unsuccessfully challenged the EPP Presidential candidate, the Frenchwoman, Nicole Fontaine. In 2002, in return for the Liberal group having supported Fontaine, the EPP backed the Liberal leader, the Irishman Pat Cox, who narrowly won the presidency from the British Labour MEP David Martin.

[9] Notably, the passage of amendments or the rejection of the position of the Council of Ministers in second and third readings of bills under the cooperation and co-decision procedures requires the support of an absolute majority of *all* MEPs, not simply among those participating in a vote.

could no longer afford ideological dogmatism if the EP was to maximize its new powers   (Kreppel 2002: 46, 36).

Overall, however, while the manner in which the EP is internally organized has certainly developed and responded to external events, it has not become any simpler. Life in the EP remains complex, and for the new MEP there will be plenty of scope for the 'surprise and sense-making' process that (as discussed in more detail in Chapter 3) socialization into a new institutional setting is generally understood to be about. Becoming an MEP means operating much of the time in an institution that is likely to be very different from any that one may have experienced at national level. And working there requires building and working with alliances that cross all national boundaries. It is quite plausible that such experiences will have a substantial impact on political actors, and that in many cases may help propel them towards an understanding and the holding of attitudes with a substantially enhanced 'European' component to them. The next section gauges MEPs' own views on whether and how this process might occur.

Experiencing life as a Member of European Parliament

As preliminary empirical research for this study, a substantial number of MEPs and former MEPs (86) were interviewed at some length (see Appendix for details). The majority were from the UK, although a number also came from several other EU member states (France, Ireland, Sweden, and Spain). Those current and former Parliamentarians spoken to were not a representative sample of MEPs, but for current purposes this is of rather minor importance. The interest for now is not with obtaining a fully representative picture—although some statistics will be quoted below, they should be interpreted with considerable caution—but more simply in conducting a 'plausibility probe' of the idea that service in the EP might lead to altered attitudinal and behavioural patterns among politicians. For these purposes, 'oversampling' among individuals from political contexts where levels of caution about European integration are relatively high— and amongst whom the scope for 'going native' might thus be expected to be greatest—is entirely appropriate.

The interviews, which were recorded and transcribed in full, were semi-structured and covered a wide range of matters, including: individuals' reasons for entering political life; their reasons for seeking candidature to the EP; and their attitudes towards various aspects of EP's institutional structures, like the operation of the committee system. But the interviews also probed the extent to which MEPs perceived learning processes and attitudinal changes to occur both in themselves and colleagues, the directions that any attitudinal change might follow, and reasons why this could happen.

Individuals' reasons for having sought to become an MEP contained a very large idiosyncratic component, related usually to the peculiarities of their personal life experiences. Nonetheless, while the early years of the elected EP appears to have attracted some who were concerned largely to advance European integration, in more recent times, the British Conservative who suggested that 'the big reason why I wanted to be an MEP, was to participate in the debate on Europe in this country... the party in this country was moving in a more Euro-sceptic direction, and I wanted to do what I could to prevent that happening'[10] seems the exception. More typical were those who appear to have seen the EP as merely one of a number of potential outlets for a political career. This finding would suggest greater scope for learning and socialization experiences to prompt attitudinal changes amongst MEPs, as it might imply that many of those entering the chamber had somewhat limited knowledge of the chamber, and maybe also possessed less than fully formed opinions about much of what the EP is concerned with.

Almost all MEPs interviewed agreed that they had undergone considerable learning about the EP, and more broadly about

[10] Interview, 8 April 1998.

European politics, as a result of their service in the chamber. As one MEP observed, 'it would be rather sad if [I] hadn't!'.[11] Questioning about the directions in which MEPs had learnt most usually led partly to a discussion of the MEP's own particular interests (often closely linked to their Parliamentary committee work) on the one hand, but on the other (frequently unprompted) to a discussion of whether their opinions had become more pro-integration. The following MEP is a particularly clear example of the link between learning and attitudinal changes:

If I use myself as an example, it's not that I actually became more pro-parliament or more pro-integrationist from a negative or lukewarm position but from almost a position of ignorance. I think a lot of politicians, even those who seek to be elected here, don't actually know that much about the institution when they arrive. And naturally you start to think about this place in the structure, once you're here, and you also start to think about the role that Europe plays and whether it's appropriate. I think by and large that does lead people to be more positive about both the parliament and the integration process. But...it's not because it suddenly becomes all in our self-interest and it's all about self-aggrandizement, I think it's just because people are educated about the system.[12]

MEPs were then questioned further about the possibility that their time in the chamber had promoted attitudinal and behavioural changes, and the reasons why this might (or might not) have occurred. Here, some important and interesting differences emerged. Although many representatives did assent to the idea of service in the chamber prompting changes, the process and underlying reasons why this was believed to have happened was understood very differently in many cases. For some MEPs, 'going native' appears to be quite simply a matter of institutional self-interest: as one French member expressed it, 'When you work somewhere that it is in your interest to say, what I'm doing here is very important. I can't see anyone not even a nationalist who would say, "yes I'm spending my time in Strasbourg but that's of

---

[11] Interview, 16 October 1998.   [12] Interview, 21 July 1999.

no importance." '[13] For others, an emphasis was placed on just 'being there'—the impact of spending substantial amounts of time in a particular, European setting. One French representative put this in particularly dramatic terms:

You take a person, take them out of their country and put them into a closed environment here, where they are going to be surrounded by EU civil servants, who tell them the same thing every morning, every afternoon and every evening; that the problems here are caused by egos and conflict between countries and that if there was a federal Europe things would be better and that the only solution is a federal Europe in the area in which they happen to be working; this ends up by sapping the intelligence of people (MEPs), not after a month but after 3, 4 or 5 years; I've seen people who have changed completely.[14]

In a more measured manner, some of the same concerns were registered by this Swedish MEP:

I think that's quite natural because here . . . you live in it every day, so what you do seems so important. Which it is, of course, but . . . you do become more pro-Europe because you see that it works. You get to know more, see how many competent people there really are here, who really try to do something, so I think that is quite natural. . . . It's very easy to become eaten up by the Brussels culture. You can spend your day writing reports and reading, and still have a bad conscience about not doing enough, and forgetting about the whole constituency.[15]

---

[13] Interview, 20 July 1999. In a rather similar vein, another French MEP suggested that 'there are people who are elected on the basis of an anti-European stance which they retain, but those who are a little hesitant and a bit open to debate take on board a European approach and realize that it is a reality and that there is real power here, and in this sense that's real progress I think' (interview 20 July 1999).

[14] Interview, 22 July 1999.

[15] Interview, 6 September 1999. Similar concerns were raised by a British MEP who talked of the 'physical dislocation from your national colleagues. It's becoming increasingly difficult to spend *any* time [in Britain]. In the European Parliament activity expands to fill the time available, and its predicted on the basis that people have nothing else to do . . . it's all designed, I think, yes I'm sure its designed, to draw people in.'

For other MEPs, however, greater emphasis was placed on the particular power of an institution, and notably the institutions of the EU, to shape the views of those working within them. As one Irish MEP, drawing on her previous experiences suggested, 'You get institutionalized apart from anything else. I'm a psychologist and I've worked in mental hospitals and I know what it's like to become institutionalized, you really do.... You do go native. You get the euro-speak'.[16] Similarly, one British representative commented

It does anywhere doesn't it? I mean, there's nothing unique about the Parliament. If you spend 10 years working for the police, your attitudes will be shifted by the environment in which you work. You can't isolate yourself from your daily surroundings.[17]

The particular potency of EU institutions in this respect was stressed, however, by some:

The magnetic attraction of it—it's very seductive once you get here, and particularly if you have any sort of position where you are mixing with any top or semi-top European positions...forever invites to dinners and all that sort of stuff...in some instances it's quite genuine changing views, and there's nothing wrong with that. You don't have to stick with the same views for ever and ever. There's nothing wrong with saying that I've learnt...but with some it's much more shallow, and they get sucked in, and before long its everything European is right.... I've seen it happen over and over again, that they have 'gone native'.[18]

Interestingly, however, while diagnosing 'going native' tendencies in colleagues, this particular MEP rejected the idea that he had been subject to the same changes himself! This was a response encountered on several occasions, stated most directly by the British Conservative who suggested regarding the idea of MEPs 'going native' that 'I think that can be observed on some of my colleagues, but I wouldn't apply it to myself'.[19] And other MEPs

[16] Interview, 2 December 1999.   [17] Interview, 9 June 1998.
[18] Interview, 8 July 1998.   [19] Interview, 3 April 1998.

went further, either accepting the idea of 'going native' only in a very moderate form, or rejecting it entirely. The following are several examples:

So people do not so much go native, but adapt to what they can rationally see to be a proper course of action.[20]

Well I think it happens in most organizations and with most individuals, I can't pretend that we're somehow immune from that assimilation process. And institutions can always assimilate individuals... [but] we are elected and I think that means the process of assimilation is much less here because we do have to go back home, we have to face the voters and therefore I think it's much more difficult to go native. Our parties have to re-select us, they're not out here, they're going to judge us from their own perspective and our voters certainly will judge us from their own perspective, in accordance with their needs.... I wouldn't say people necessarily go native here. Otherwise, for example, I think the parliament would have been far more loyal to the Commission earlier this year than it has shown. The pattern in the last twenty years is we've become more able to criticize and hold the Commission to account. If we'd gone native I think we wouldn't have done what we did earlier in the year.[21]

I was maybe a bit more idealistic about Europe 4 years ago than I am now. I do think that we've taken on a lot in trying to get 15 countries to work together: I'm more conscious now of the difficulties than perhaps I was. It doesn't make me cynical about Europe: it makes me more realistic... anybody who thinks that we are all seduced by the *foie gras* in Strasbourg—forget it.... I know you hear the expression 'going native' but its not very intelligent.[22]

Well, if it's true, then its more true of Members of the Commission than of Parliament. I'm thinking of Lord Cockfield and Leon Brittan, both pretty sceptical of Europe before they went there; both became extremely pro-European. But what they don't have, which MEPs do have, is regular contact with their constituencies. And I think that this acts as quite a serious break on your, er, on the chances of you 'going native'. And my feeling on the whole is that people—there were a lot of people of course who went into the European Parliament—people like Derek Prag, Peter Price, Bill Newton-Dunn (although he seems to have changed his attitude

---

[20] Interview, 21 July 1999.   [21] Ibid.   [22] Interview, 23 July 1998.

now), they were all *intensely* committed to an integrated, federal Europe, proportional representation and all. So they had gone native before they arrived. I don't know that the European Parliament—I know an awful lot of people like Eric Forth who if anything went in the other direction. And I think the reason for that is that people have this counterbalance with the constituencies.[23]

This question of 'going native'—it's a peculiarly absurd idea, isn't it?[24]

As can be seen, when questioned directly about the idea that service in an EU institution like the EP prompts changes in their attitudes and behaviours, MEPs can and do differ in their reactions. Of the eighty-six MEPs interviewed, thirty-six (or 42 per cent of the sample), clearly agreed with this notion; another twelve (14 per cent) indicated agreement in a mild or more am-biguous form; 28 per cent (twenty-four MEPs) appeared to have mixed or uncertain views; while fourteen MEPs (16 per cent of the sample) indicated clear disagreement. The balance of opinion among those MEPs interviewed was thus favourable towards the 'going native' hypothesis, but this balance of opinion was far from overwhelming. Furthermore, there are a number of reasons why we cannot simply take MEPs' word for it: why the evidence that can be drawn from interviewing them should not be regarded as definitive. These reasons, and their further implications, are con-sidered in detail in the concluding section.

The need for further study

The first two sections of this chapter have discussed, respectively, the development of the EP within the institutional structures of the EU, and the internal organization of the EP. The discussion in both sections reinforced the plausibility of the idea that service in the EP might incline political actors towards becoming more pro-integration in their attitudes and behaviours: this hypothesis is consistent both with how the EP has behaved col-lectively in pushing consistently for greater powers, and also with

[23] Interview, 11 November 1998.   [24] Interview, 8 April 1998.

a recognition of the complexity and unfamiliarity of the political environment that most new MEPs will encounter when entering the institution. The third section of the chapter then went on to demonstrate that many EP members themselves accept the notion that they tend to 'go native' over time.

The case for the hypothesis that a pervasive 'going native' process operates on members of the EU's elected institution might, thus, seem to be already quite securely established. But the argument of this concluding section of the chapter is that such a secure grounding is more illusory than real; and that substantial further study is needed. There are several aspects to this argument.

The first, most simple, and least far-reaching point is that the interview evidence presented above was drawn from an unrepresentative sample of current or past MEPs. As was discussed earlier, a biased sample is of fairly minimal importance for an initial probe of the plausibility of an idea, but it assumes much greater significance if we want our evidence to help deliver a more definitive conclusion. At the very least, evidence that is more representative of the balance of experiences and opinions in the EP would be required to help reach such a conclusion.

A second point, of more substantial concern, is that the interview evidence presented above gave a far from clear picture as to the reasons why institutional socialization in the EP, or other EU institutions, might be apparently so powerful in shaping attitudes and behaviours. A number of possible reasons were suggested, but none dominated the interviews conducted: the overall impression is that among MEPs who believe that they do tend to 'go native', the driving forces are seen as some combination of learning, self-interest and physical dislocation from the national political environment. But the precise nature of this combination is far from clear. This should come as no surprise. Most MEPs are busy political actors, who one would presume—and, indeed, generally hope—have more pressing things to do with their time than engage in intellectually precise theorizing. Scholars should not expect those whom they study to do their most important work for them. But this does point to the need for a clear theoretical understanding of why socialization processes in an institution like the EP might be expected to work in certain directions; as well as consideration of why such forces might not work as powerfully as some expect. This challenge is taken up in Chapters 3 and 4.

A third point, already mentioned briefly in Chapter 1, is that the in-depth, semi-structured interview has some generic problems as a methodology for investigating institutional socialization processes. A first problem here concerns the honesty of responses, and the possibility that many respondents are tempted to give what they consider to be 'socially desirable' responses. To some degree this is a problem facing all attitudinal research. But it may be of particular concern where, as in the investigation here, one is treading on politically very sensitive ground. The language of 'going native' was clearly familiar to most MEPs who were interviewed, and some of those indicating disagreement with the underlying concept appeared to object to what is, in many political quarters, highly pejorative terminology. If a degree of defensive self-justification does enter into responses to questions in this are, this suggests that the evidence gathered from interviews may tend to *underestimate* socialization effects.

An alternative possibility, however, is that the very familiarity of the terminology associated with the underlying idea of institutional socialization may lead many individuals to *overinterpret* evidence. If it is already widely believed that there is a tendency for actors within these institutional settings to become socialized in a particular direction, then it is quite possible that people will ascribe many observed behaviours among others as examples of the impact of effective socialization, when such behaviours might reasonably be subject to other possible interpretations.

A third highly important point on the value of interview evidence in this context is that interview questions about socialization effects are likely to place very heavy, and almost certainly quite unreasonable, interpretative burdens on those being interviewed. The point here is that where one asks individuals directly whether the attitudes or behaviours of either themselves or others have changed over time as a result of institutional socialization

processes, the scholar is essentially asking respondents simultaneously to do *all* of the following:

1. Make their own estimate of the value of the dependent variable
   at the present (time, t);
2. Make an estimate of the value of the dependent variable in
   the—possibly quite distant—past (time, $t - 1$), with all the at-
   tendant problems of recall biases that are thereby implied; and
3. To estimate the relative power of a particular causal mechanism—institutional socialization—in explaining any differences
   in the value of the dependent variable at t and $t - 1$ compared
   to the relative power of any other causal mechanisms.

It will be difficult for even the most well-intentioned interviewee
to give accurate responses to such questions—indeed, it will probably be difficult for them even to know what an accurate response
would be. A point made above is relevant once again: scholars
should not expect others to do their most important work for
them.

The overall conclusion to be drawn is that, in the context of a
study of institutional socialization, information gained from
interviews constitutes a rather weak and impressionistic type of
evidence. As will be seen in Chapter 3, much previous work in this
area has focused on investigating individuals' impressions of attitudinal or behavioural changes—their own or that of others.
While such information is useful, it is certainly a weaker type of
evidence than more direct measures of those attitudes and behaviours themselves. It is, after all, quite possible that people's impressions of their own—and even more their impressions of other
peoples'—attitudes and behaviours are simply wrong. Where possible we should seek for direct, independent evidence that any
posited changes have actually occurred: this means drawing on
sources of data that measures the attitudes and behaviours that we
are actually interested in.

In short, the interview evidence and discussion presented so far
cannot be taken as the last word on the subject that this study is
concerned with. Further empirical work is clearly needed; so also

is likely to be theoretical clarification of the issues at stake. But preceding that must first come a discussion that makes clear what is known about the role of socialization processes in shaping the attitudes and behaviours of those serving in EU institutions—and, by implication, what has not yet been established. This will be the task for the next chapter.

3

Going Native?

This chapter lays the groundwork for the rest of the study by establishing what we already know about the subject—and clarifying what we do not know. This is a more complicated task than it might initially appear, because while there is little systematic research directly investigating socialization processes within EU bodies, a vast amount of literature in some way or another touches on the issue. What follows, therefore, is necessarily wide ranging. The first section of the chapter examines the variety of 'going native'-type arguments that exist in both popular and academic discussion of the EU, highlighting those instances that focus specifically on the EP, and also noting that such ideas can be seen to reflect prominent themes within broader academic literatures in the disciplines of sociology, organizational psychology and political science. But in the second section of the chapter it is shown that very little evidence has actually been found to support the hypothesized changes in political actors' attitudes and behaviours linked to their service within EU bodies. Rather, empirical investigations have generally produced negative or 'null' findings. In the final section of the chapter, therefore, two possible resolutions of this conflict between hypotheses and evidence are explored: that defects in previous empirical research explain the absence of evidence in support of socialization effects; or that such hypotheses are based on mistaken or inappropriate theoretical premises.

Going native?

It seems to me immaterial, which party to vote for in the coming European elections, since as soon as they get elected they immediately 'go native' and see it as their job to represent the EU rather than their electors in this country. Would it be impertinent of me to suggest that they should promote the interests of this country, which are not always synonymous with those of the EU?[1]

Even those candidates who claim to be Euro-sceptics will soon have it knocked out of them after a few weeks *sur le continent*. A Christian Democrat in Brussels told me this week: 'If you're a Tory involved in European politics and legislation you can't keep saying "I don't go along with any of this", because it gets too boring. All MEPs eventually go native.'[2]

An objective observer must conclude that a corporate spirit born of working together and the awareness of participating in an ambitious historic enterprise have created and maintained among the Communities' functionaries a prevailing European loyalty.   (Spinelli 1996)

The notion that those who work in European institutions come to develop a more 'European' outlook is one of the most widespread conjectures made about the EU. Such ideas permeated normative writings pre-dating the beginnings of the EU. Many of the earliest advocates of European unity contended that working together in such a context would generate new, shared understandings among those participating.[3] David Mitrany's functionalism similarly imagined cooperative efforts developing new levels of international understanding and altered political beliefs (in the direction of reducing mutual hostility).[4] It is less clear whether similar notions were important for the EU's founders. But the first analysts who went to study the new European enterprise were more definite. The complex neofunctionalist synthesis of Ernst

---

[1] *The Times*, 7 June 1999, Letters Page.

[2] *The Guardian* (G2 section p. 5), 2 June 1999, Francis Wheen column.

[3] For a review, see Rich (1996).

[4] For instance: 'Each of us is in fact a bundle of functional loyalties; so that to build a world community upon such a conception is merely to extend and consolidate it also between national societies and groups' (Mitrany 1946: 204).

Haas included, as one of its core elements, a theory of socialization—the idea that interactions occurring within new contexts can lead to changed attitudes:

> As the process of integration proceeds, it is assumed that values will undergo change, that interests will be redefined in terms of a regional, rather than a purely national orientation.   (Haas 1968: 13)

Haas's very definition of the integration process encompassed attitude and loyalty shifts on the part of political actors: the ultimate achievement of the integration process, the development of a 'political community', would mean 'a condition in which specific groups and individuals show more loyalty to their central political institutions than to any other political authority, in a specific period of time and in a definable geographic space' (Haas 1968: 5). These transfers of loyalty would occur, initially at least, mainly among political and socio-economic elites: for many of the latter this would be prompted by the altered locus for provision of their functional needs, but for those within the newly established European institutions this process was seen as essentially a straightforward consequence of the development of shared values within the new environment.[5]

Haas's thinking on socialization overlapped marginally with that of Karl Deutsch, though the latter was concerned more with broader social interactions generating a 'bottom-up' process leading to the development of a sense of 'community' that included 'we-feeling' and 'mutual sympathy and loyalty' (e.g. Deutsch 1966) with regard to the basic idea that more frequent interactions can

---

[5] Or, as Haas put it, for 'decision-makers in the new institutions', 'the heterogeneity of their origins may compel them to fashion doctrines and develop codes of conduct which represent an amalgamation of various national belief systems or group values' (Haas 1968: 19). O'Neill explains that 'The sociological consequences of the elite transactions which are the core of the neo-functionalist notion of political change were assumed to be both sufficiently cumulative and intrusive to erode over time any exclusive sense of national identity. In short, a cultural osmosis is assumed to be at work in the fabric of these European societies participating in the Community endeavour' (1996: 43).

alter attitudes and even promote elements of a common identity. Refinements of neofunctionalism by Leon Lindberg and Philippe Schmitter gave significant theoretical weight to socialization processes on participants, and the development of 'community-mindedness' among them (Lindberg 1963, 1965, 1966; Schmitter 1971: 864–5). For these early theorists, as Pollack (1998: 13) summarizes, 'Regarding the mechanism of attitude change among these elites, we find . . . references to socialization into a certain Community "code" as a result of prolonged experience of cooperation.'[6]

The idea that socialization processes within EU institutions tend to shape individuals' identities and attitudes in a more 'European' direction has, however, by no means remained unique to neofunctionalism. Such ideas have become prevalent in many different areas of writing about the EU. Mass media coverage of the EU is replete with references to those at the European level 'going native'—or expressing similar ideas in less pejorative terms.[7] Much of the general contemporary academic literature on EU institutions and policymaking appears to assume that those participating in the institutions are subject to a significant degree of socialization into shared norms and values (e.g. Armstrong and Bulmer 1997; Cini 1996: 222–3; Hayes-Renshaw and Wallace 1997: 235).[8] And scholarly projects that build on the

[6] Similarly, Corbett (1998: 48) points out that neo-functionalists saw those in the EP as 'developing habits of behaviour at the supranational level'. It should be noted that references to Pollack (1998) are to an unpublished conference paper made available through the internet; page references are to the version possessed by this author, and may differ from copies of the paper available elsewhere.

[7] To give but two examples: a *Daily Telegraph* interview with Sir Leon (now Lord) Brittan after his completion of term as European Commissioner, observed that 'He insists that he travelled to what his countrymen increasingly regard as the heart of darkness without going native' (1 February 2000, Alice Thomson, p. 23). Another example, taken from press coverage after the Cardiff June 1998 European Council summit, is this: 'The idea of a super-council of deputy prime ministers raises more questions than it answers. There is a clear tendency for those personally engaged in Europe to go native', Martin Walker, 'Analysis: balancing act in the rise and rise of neo-nation states', *Guardian*, 17 June 1998.

[8] Other work, though not making such blanket assumptions, still raises the issue of socialization as something to be considered: see, for example, Duff (1994).

intellectual tradition of social constructivism—which, after achieving prominence in International Relations theory (e.g. Wendt 1992, 1999; Hopf 2002) has recently been applied to analysis of the EU (e.g. Christiansen et al. 1999)—have developed not a dissimilar position, focusing on the 'mutually constitutive, non-instrumental bases of social interaction', and viewing the EU as a potential venue for 'complex social learning, a process whereby agent interests and identities are shaped through and during interaction' (Checkel 2001a: 556, 561). Constructivist-inspired work has tended to posit both 'macro' and 'micro' processes of attitude changes—the former concerning the ability of EU to reshape the preferences of member states, and the latter considering, as one possible micro-foundation of the former, the socialization of individual political actors operating in EU institutions.[9]

In summary, the belief that individuals are socialized within European institutions towards generally more pro-European attitudes is widely held. This is equally true for the more specific body of work on the EP. The question of socialization effects had been explored during the era of the non-elected Parliament, when the pertinent question was whether national MPs had their attitudes influenced by their part-time service in the assembly. Would their horizons be broadened, and their beliefs changed? Early work, particularly that of Kerr (1973), indicated that this was not, generally, what occurred (see later). The issue began to be raised once more with particular force, however, when direct election of MEPs finally happened in 1979, and the prospect loomed of a mostly full-time and perhaps power hungry, elected chamber. Marquand (1979: 70–7) argued that those elected with more sceptical views about integration would find it difficult to resist the Euro-federalist ethos that would dominate the Parliament. Meanwhile, Cotta suggested that, along with a general inclination in favour of a closer European union, a more specific aspiration would develop among MEPs—towards making

---

[9] On the latter point, see Checkel (2001a); Jachtenfuchs et al. (1998: 411).

the Parliament itself a powerful lawmaking body within that union:

We now have for the first time a political elite that is not based in national political institutions but in a supranational institution. A political class that has therefore a vested interest in the strengthening of the European parliament and more broadly in the promotion of European integration (Cotta 1984: 126).

Subsequent developments appeared to support Cotta. In the following years, the EP consistently championed both closer European unity and enhanced powers for itself; meanwhile, some evidence did suggest that a distinct 'Euro-elite' was developing within the Parliament. For instance, Westlake (1994) analysed the development of a more pro-European outlook amongst Britain's elected MEPs, finding that while a significant proportion of the first UK contingent (particularly from the Labour party) were hostile to European unity, this soon began to change. The British Labour Group transmuted into the European Parliamentary Labour Party, its development of a more positive attitude towards the EU preceding similar changes in the views of the domestic party. Conservative MEPs, meanwhile, generally retained a positive attitude even as their domestic party became ever more 'Eurosceptic'. It seemed, therefore, that service in the chamber had contributed to more pro-European views among British MEPs.[10]

---

[10] It is unclear, however, what interpretation can be placed upon such trends. Behavioural evidence is examined by Westlake, but the results are inconclusive. He examines the voting patterns of the British contingent across fourteen votes, between 1981 and 1992, where issues concerning greater powers for the EP and closer European unity were placed before MEPs (Westlake 1994: 245–57). The major method of analysis, however, is to chart *aggregate* patterns of support, opposition or abstention/absence across these fourteen votes. Not only is there no identifiable trend in support among UK members across the votes (charting aggregate levels of support over time reveals a statistically insignificant coefficient); even if there were, it would be difficult to draw any clear inferences from such a pattern. Increasing British support could have come from the changing attitudes of UK members in the chamber (although in fact, charting simply the behaviour of surviving members of the 1979 intake across all fourteen votes yields little evidence of a trend either), *or* from less supportive members in this original cohort gradually being replaced by more supportive figures.

The intuitive plausibility of the idea that MEPs, working together regularly in a European chamber, should come to adopt a
similar, pro-European viewpoint, has to many authors been so
strong that they have been willing to assert it as correct without
actually testing it.[11] Featherstone (1979: 102–3), for instance, posited a rudimentary model of the socialization process believed to
occur among MEPs. Several factors—exposure to new information; 'continuous contact with foreign colleagues'; the assumption of non-national roles; new structures of work; and exposure
to new group norms and pressures—were believed to make
European parliamentarians, among other things, both more
knowledgeable about European issues and 'in some cases, also
more amenable to [the] Community idea'. However, as with
later work, little evidence was presented to support these hypotheses.[12] In a more recent study, Johanssen (1995: 19), who observes
that 'MEPs form part of a massive transnational socialization
process', and notes the link between his work and neofunctionalist ideas, states:

If an MEP was not committed to European integration when entering
Parliament a Euro-mindedness is likely to evolve over time, reflecting a
process of socialization and the mere fact that he or she, as a co-legislator
engaged in transnational activity, is destined to widen personal horizons
beyond purely national interests.   (Johanssen 1995: 21)[13]

---

[11] Among the numerous examples are: 'very probably, new MEPs will soon be
socialized into this consensual style of politics, thus largely allaying fears that
inexperience may render cooperation more difficult' (Boyce 1995: 151); see also
Abeles (1992: 315), Corbett et al. (1995: 300), Dunphy (1996: 142), Hagger and Wing
(1979: 183), Hrbek (1990: 177), Kirchner (1984: 52), Jackson (1993: 169) and Marsh and
Wessels (1997: 238). Pappamikail (1998: 208) suggests similar developments among
British Labour MEPs, but more cautiously.

[12] The only significant supporting evidence adduced by Featherstone is qualitative interviews where several MEPs observe apparent changes of mind among
initially anti-European Labour members.

[13] The same author also quotes the work of Kerr (1973: 71) stating that MEPs
'who enter the European Parliament for the first time are exposed to a set of
parliamentary traditions and norms which place an exceedingly high value on a
strong commitment to regional integration', but unfortunately fails to mention

Such statements are rendered plausible by being broadly consistent with traditions of thinking in several academic disciplines. The notion of encounters with new organizational surroundings provoking attitudinal, behavioural and cognitive changes is widely regarded as one of the most strongly supported findings within the field of organizational psychology (for reviews, see Falcione and Wilson 1988; Feldman 1981; Louis 1980; Ostroff and Kozlowski 1992). As van Maanen and Schein (1979: 210) observe, 'research has yet to discover a work setting which leaves people unmarked by their participation'. Within social psychology, Herbert Kelman has emphasized how contact between individuals of disparate backgrounds and views can prompt sometimes dramatic reappraisals of the images held of those from other countries, and how through working together,

individuals and groups from different countries become committed to international cooperation not as an abstract value, but as a concrete vehicle.... They become involved in a network of interdependent individuals and groups, without references to national differences, and are likely to develop a sense of loyalty to it.   (Kelman 1966: 575)[14]

that Kerr's findings offer little support to a socialization hypothesis. In other work, Ovey, who draws from elements of the 'new governance' school in seeking to understand MEPs' work of the parliament, is also fairly definitive: 'The formal and informal rules which guide preferences and behaviour are discovered upon entry to an institution, are transmitted through socialisation and are embedded in normative orders.... The institution thus provides "the lenses through which actors view the world" (Powell and DiMaggio 1991: 13), exerts pressure on values and preferences, shapes ideas and attitudes and accordingly leads to an identification with the institution' (Ovey 2000: 4). Note that institutional identification is not put forward as a hypothesis, but is stated more or less definitively. The same author later suggests 'The European Parliament influences MEPs and affects their identities' (Ovey 2000: 7) and states that 'MEPs respond to the institutional framework of the EP, embedded in the norms of the political system of the EU, by unintentionally becoming detached from national parties' (Ovey 2000: 8). Although supporting citations are made to the general institutional literature (March and Olsen 1989; Powell and DiMaggio 1991), no actual empirical evidence is deployed by Ovey in support of these contentions.

[14] For a study that applies some of Kelman's ideas to the EU, see Hewstone (1985). A more general review of the psychology of attitude changes is given in Zimbardo and Leippe (1991).

In a roughly analogous manner, a long-standing tradition in sociology has emphasized the power of 'institutional cultures' within organizations to shape the views of members: this tradition has been manifested notably, and recently, in the sociological variant of the 'new institutionalism'. In this school, the impact of institutional socialization processes on individuals appears sometimes to be not only powerful, but also more or less inevitable (e.g. March and Olsen 1989: 22, 48, 160; Jepperson 1991: 146; Thelen and Steinmo 1992: 27). Institutions themselves are seen as 'normative vessels': carriers of an institutional culture that encompasses not only knowledge, but also beliefs and values.

Moving rather closer to the EP, the political science literature on legislatures and parliaments also includes a significant body of research appearing to demonstrate the ability of parliamentary chambers to inculcate members into core values, beliefs, and practices. Fenno's classic work (1962, 1973) on the Appropriations Committee in the US House of Representatives showed experienced members exerting considerable pressure upon neophyte legislators to at least comply with established practices, if not support them. Other scholars of the US Congress have examined the issue both from the point of view of the chamber—how the legislature must 'transmit its norms to legislative newcomers in order to insure the continued, unaltered operation of the institution' (Asher 1973: 499)—and from that of the new Member of Congress 'They must learn to make sense of this new world and understand their place in it—in short, become socialized in a new institution and role' (Fiellen 1962: 80; see also Bell and Price 1975; Matthews 1960).[15] The dependent variables examined in this body of work vary considerably across different types of attitudes and behaviours. In some instances, the emphasis is on learning particular

---

[15] In a similar manner, Hagle (1993), writing about the experiences of new members of the US Supreme Court, supports the idea that new members of political institutions undergo periods of learning and socialization: rather like much of the organizational psychology work mentioned below, Hagle sees new entrants undergoing an initial period of 'bewilderment and disorientation'.

norms within the institution; in others, legislative socialization is seen to have a more clearly 'political' impact in promoting political conservatism. Thus, Searing's study (1986) of the British House of Commons shows membership of the chamber tending, over time, to moderate opinion, both on matters of socio-economic policy and on questions on radical institutional and political reform; while Mughan et al. (1997) map declining institutional radicalism among Labour members in the 1980s, even on the relatively moderate reform measure of televising the Parliament. The pattern seems to hold in France as well:

Changes in political attitudes are a well-known phenomenon. It has often been said that in France a deputy begins his political career at the extreme left, to end on the right. A traditional joke . . . could be translated: 'Sonny, when choosing a deputy, do take the most red because he will lose his color!'   (Prost and Rosenveig 1977: 102)[16]

Previous empirical research

The previous section demonstrated the prevalence of notions that EU institutions, including the EP, socialize individuals into more pro-European attitudes and behaviours. It further demonstrated that such ideas are plausible for having parallels with work conducted in other contexts. This section will consider the results of previous empirical studies that have sought to test these ideas.

Relevant previous empirical research falls into two categories: a substantial, though disparate, body of work on various International Organizations (including the EU), and a much

---

[16] For other discussions of legislative socialization, see *inter alia* Clark and Price (1977), Kornberg and Thomas (1965). It should, of course, be noted that the literature on parliamentary socialization usually points to two effects of this process: (i) Representatives coming to learn the norms and prevailing values of the parliament; and (ii) A general political 'deradicalization' effect. Such effects cannot be assumed to be the same as socialization into greater pro-integrationism. (I am grateful to an anonymous reader of the manuscript for clarifying this point to me.)

more limited set of previous studies focusing on the EP.[17] Among studies of participants in International Organizations, Alger's work (1963) on national delegates to the UN General Assembly, drawing on interviews with twenty-five delegates from different countries, found solid evidence of cognitive changes—participants became much more informed about the UN and global problems. But he detected no similar *attitudinal* changes in the direction of greater support for the UN or for international cooperation. Alger's findings were echoed by other work, such as Jacobson's study (1967) of members of three international assemblies, Pendergast's work (1976) on Italian and French officials in EU Permanent Representations, and Bonham's research into Scandinavian delegates to multinational assemblies. The latter concluded:

The results of this research do not support the hypothesis that participation in international assemblies alters the attitudes of the delegates.... Delegates to the Consultative Assembly supported political integration more strongly than non-participants, but it is likely that this difference was a consequence of their more favourable initial attitudes than their experiences in the Assembly... recruitment, rather than participation, is a better explanation for the attitudes held by those who participate in regional assemblies.   (Bonham 1970: 335–6)

Two important issues are raised here. The first is that where institutional experiences do prompt attitudinal changes among participants in international organizations, these appear often to be in terms of inducing a greater sense of 'realism' (see also Smith 1973); both previous outright hostility and idealistic support seem to be moderated, and participants 'regress to the mean'.[18] Second, any

---

[17] My review of the general literature here draws in several instances on that of Pollack (1998).

[18] The regression to the mean effect is also found by Riggs (1977), studying the speeches of delegates to the UN General Assembly from the US Congress; Karns (1977) produces almost identical findings by looking at foreign policy roll-call voting records (see also Riggs and Mykletun 1979; Peck 1979).

greater support for international cooperation observed among delegates to international fora may well not come about because of socialization processes, but follows from 'self-selection', that is those who volunteer for service in international institutions being disproportionately supportive of international cooperation before such experiences. Gareau's study (1978) of Senators and Representatives from the US Congress who served as UN delegates was consistent with this self-selection explanation; these findings were further endorsed by Riggs and Mykletun (1979). The fascinating anthropological work on EC officials reported by Bellier (1997: 104) also suggests that self-selection is important in shaping attitudes.

The most systematic, theoretically rigorous and ambitious work conducted in this area in recent years has been that by Jeffrey Checkel (2001a, 2001b, 2003). Checkel sees 'going native' effects as being a consequences of the process of 'argumentative persuasion', through which people can come to altered views, and even changed understandings of core interests.[19] Showing a degree of rigour missing in much other work, Checkel also develops a set of specific hypotheses concerning when argumentative persuasion is likely to be more (or less) effective. However, this work has still been subject to severe theoretical criticism. Not only are some of Checkel's hypotheses difficult to operationalize in a falsifiable manner; in addition, Checkel regards his hypotheses as following directly from social-constructivist metatheoretical premises, and yet Andrew Moravcsik has shown that equivalent notions to most or all of his hypotheses could well be derived from mainstream rationalist research traditions (Moravcsik 2001). But most importantly for our current purposes, in his study of committees in the Council of Europe, Checkel finds only very weak

---

[19] As with other social constructivist authors working in this area (e.g. Risse 2000) Checkel's emphasis on persuasion draws on the broader ideas of Jurgen Habermas, specifically Habermas's notions of 'Communicative Action'.

and partial evidence of socialization effects actually occurring (Checkel 2003: 224–5).

Three studies of EU institutions have been among those few claiming some support for a socialization hypothesis. However, these works have all suffered from methodological defects that render any supportive conclusions dubious.[20] Bellier (1997) examines 'Conversion from the National into the European' among EC officials. However, hard evidence of attitudinal changes in such a direction (beyond self-reports by officials) is conspicuously lacking. Similar observations can be made about the study of Lewis (1998): examining officials in the EU's Committee of Permanent Representatives (Coreper), he discusses 'Supranationality as a Shared Value' (pp. 489–90), but again is entirely dependent on self-reports of attitudinal changes, rather than any independent measure. Trondal's work (2001) examines officials participating in Commission Expert Committees and Working Parties. However, even the modest 'enactment of supranational allegiances' (2001: 15) claimed is based on officials' *perceptions* of an *esprit de corps* in committees, and of the EC being an independent supranational actor. Thus, Trondal's evidence is not even that of self-reports, but reports of the perceptions of others' attitudes. The more methodologically sound work of Hooghe (1999a, 1999b, 2001) on officials in the EC, which conceptualizes and seeks to measure 'socialization' with far greater clarity and care, than is done in most other work, finds little sign of significant attitudinal changes that can be linked to socialization at the EU level. Specifically, while Hooghe suggests that socialization is often important for shaping attitudes, it is more commonly pre-entry socialization outside the EC that seems to matter. She thus concludes:

The widespread assumption that the Commission is a greenhouse for supranationalism has little basis in reality. It is *not* the case that the longer

---

[20] Pollack (1998) provides an extended discussion of methodological problems in studies of other International Organizations.

one works in the Commission, the more supranationalist one becomes. (Hooghe 2001: 209)[21]

Overall, two things are striking about the findings of this body of work. The first is the consistency of the findings, despite their being conducted in somewhat varying contexts and with different methods. Little sound evidence of socialization effects has been found. The second notable point is the stark contrast between these findings and the expectations generated earlier in this chapter.

Is the situation any different for European Parliamentarians? After all, if parliaments really are the powerful socializing influences they have often been suggested to be, it could still be the case that a 'going native' effect works for MEPs. The first serious work speaking to this concern was that of Haas. Interestingly, however, while believing that socialization processes were an important aspect of the integration story elsewhere, Haas found little evidence of this among members of the then Common Assembly. The reason for this was simple:

Very few, if any, individual members were persuaded to the federalist creed as a result of their work in Strasbourg. With the exception of perhaps fifteen members, *the bulk was more or less in favour of integration before they ever took up their supranational mandate.*   (Haas 1968: 437, emphasis added)

In short, we see self-selection again: the voluntaristic nature of service in the Common Assembly tended to act as a magnet for those already positive towards the building of 'Europe', and who perhaps saw service in the chamber as a contribution to European unity. For the most part, only confirmed Euro-enthusiasts bothered expending time and energy undertaking part-time service in the virtually powerless European chamber. Those who did choose to do so might

---

[21] Summarizing her findings across a number of attitudinal dimensions, Hooghe concludes that 'contexts external to the Commission are more decisive for preferences than are contexts within the Commission...the results are unambiguous: external influences are much stronger than experiences within the Commission' (Hooghe 2001: 213).

perhaps, through their interactions with fellow delegates to the Assembly, reinforce their pro-European attitudes. But service in Strasbourg was unlikely to promote any fundamental attitude shifts.

Other early work on the EP supported Haas's argument. Kerr's study (1973) of a sample of French and German MEPs suggested that longer-serving members developed a more sophisticated understanding of European politics (in other words, the sort of cognitive development discussed above), but he could detect little evidence of any substantial changes in attitudes towards either integration or the specific status of the EP. When compared with samples of their fellow national legislators,[22] MEPs attitudes were more 'pro-European', but they were no less so amongst new-comers to the EP than with veterans of several years' experience. This led Kerr (1973: 45) to speak of 'the self-recruitment of many legislators who were avowed Europeans before their nomination'.[23]

This analysis, however, was based on a small number of interviews, among MEPs from only two countries (albeit two large and important EU member states), and was conducted at a time when the EP's membership was unelected and the chamber virtually powerless. Thus, Kerr's conclusions could hardly be treated as definitive. Unfortunately, there has been little empirical research following up these lines of enquiry since the first direct elections in 1979; moreover, as documented above, much subsequent writing on the EP has tended to *assume* the existence of strong socialization effects among elected MEPs, rather than investigate the matter. The body of empirical studies is thus limited. A paper by Brzinski et al. (1998), in testing for various sources of dissent from the whip of party groups in the 1994–9 EP, attempted to tap

---

[22] Kerr's study was conducted, of course, on the pre-1979 unelected EP, whose membership was made up of national legislators delegated to serve in Strasbourg.

[23] In another study conducted prior to direct elections for the EP, Feld and Wildgen (1975) found that few of eighteen national MPs whom they interviewed who had also had served as MEPs believed that their European experience had made their attitudes more 'pro-European'.

socialization effects in a multivariate statistical analysis of voting patterns in the chamber, as one potential source of variation in party cohesion levels.[24] The empirical analysis is rather under-developed: potential socialization effects are tapped only by a dichotomous measure (freshman MEP or not). As with other work, the study finds high aggregate levels of cohesion (cf. Hix and Lord 1997; Kreppel 2002; Raunio 1997) amidst considerable individual-level variation; this variation is partly explained by nationality (those from countries that joined the EU later were more likely to defect) and by committee membership (there were some effects, though not consistent ones, for committee members to defect on subjects close to their committee), but not at all by time spent in the chamber. The authors thus conclude, 'it appears that socialization into the European parliament has little effect on party discipline' (Brzinski et al. 1998: 23).

In other work, Scully (1998, 2002) has investigated whether length of service in the EP is associated with support for closer integration as measured through voting behaviour on several key votes in the EP in recent times. The consistent pattern, obtaining across all the votes analysed, is that longer-serving members are *not* systematically more likely to endorse pro-integrationist positions.[25] Similar null findings pervade two chapters in a recent edited volume (Katz and Wessels 1999). Katz (1999: 43), discussing attitudinal differences between MEPs and members of national parliaments, claims that '[i]n part they reflect socialization into the norms of the institutions', despite providing little evidence to support this contention. When he tests for the impact of length of tenure in the institution on MEPs' attitudes over several key issues, Katz (1999: 34–9) finds longer-serving members to be no

---

[24] The method used to assess socialization effects is a dummy variable inserted into their multivariate equations, for whether an MEP is a 'freshman' or not. The authors suggest: 'A longer membership in the European Parliament should be associated with more party cohesion' (Brzinski et al. 1998: 17).

[25] Similar findings are also reported by Bailer and Schneider (2000) in examining MEP's behaviour on divisions relating to the enlargement policy of the EU.

more likely than others to adopt a pro-integration or pro-parliament line.

Likewise, a chapter by Franklin and Scarrow (1999), which draws on data derived from surveys of current MEPs and candidates in the 1994 EP elections, measures attitudes towards the EU at two separate points in time—in 1994 and (among some of those elected) in 1996. The study is severely limited—as the authors fully acknowledge—by the small number of respondents common to both surveys ($N = 43$), the fact that they were from only two countries (Germany and the Netherlands), and that they were able to conduct measures at only two, widely separated, time points. Nonetheless, the results of this study are consistent with those of others reported here: the authors find, at best, only very marginal evidence in support of socialization effects operating in the expected direction, and they conclude that 'MEPs are very like national MPs' (Franklin and Scarrow 1999: 58).[26]

Thus, the main conclusion we can draw from the limited research on the EP is one essentially consistent with the findings of the wider literature. That empirical work which has been conducted has confounded widely held hypotheses regarding the socializing power of international institutions in general, and EU institutions, including the EP, in particular. These findings have been obtained, moreover, despite the apparently strong basis for those hypotheses. We therefore arrive at a serious puzzle: why have the results of empirical research so consistently contradicted expectations? In the concluding section of the chapter, potential resolutions of this puzzle are considered.

Reconciling theory and evidence

When a hypothesis that appears to have a strong theoretical basis behind it fails to be confirmed by the examination of empirical

---

[26] The same chapter also finds (pp. 54–5) little or no electoral effect (in terms of pro-Europeans being more likely to be elected), and little difference in attitudes when the possibility of 'cohort effects' among longer-serving MEPs is considered.

evidence, two broad types of potential explanation would appear to exist: either our original theory is wrong, or our analysis of the evidence is wrong. That is, our theoretical conceptualization of a phenomenon may require recasting in some way in order to explain our empirical findings; or, alternatively, measurement error, insufficiencies of data, the incorrect application of particular analytical techniques and/or simple misinterpretation of results could mean that previous empirical work has produced erroneous findings. This final section of the chapter will consider whether either of these possibilities can explain the absence of evidence to support hypotheses concerning the socializing power of EU and other international institutions.

Empirically wrong?

There can be little justification for the position of some of the work reviewed above: that is to *assume* that particular (and important) developments occur, yet fail to use available empirical evidence to verify such assumptions.[27] However, such scholarly practices are so obviously wrong-headed that they surely deserve little further consideration. Of more urgent importance is to consider whether that empirical work which has been conducted may have gone seriously awry.

The literature on international organizations reviewed above is certainly not flawless. As Pollack (1998) observes, most of the numerous studies conducted have been guilty of one or more of the following methodological 'sins': failure to allow for proper comparisons between those who have experience of international organizations and those who have not had such experiences; failure to allow for self-selection, election and/or selective exiting effects (i.e. those putting themselves forward, getting chosen

---

[27] Pollack, for instance, observes in much of the constructivist-inspired literature on the EU 'a tendency among constructivists to *assume* the existence of certain phenomena ... such as identity or preference change, as the starting point for analysis, and consequently to reject rationalist approaches for their purported inability to predict and explain these phenomena' (2001: 234–5, emphasis in original).

and/or seeking to remain in an institution being systematically different from those who fall by the wayside at one of these stages); and failure properly to chart change (or its absence) over time, perhaps by taking measures of attitudes or behaviours that give only limited potential insight into the possible effects of institutional socialization processes.

Nonetheless, while individual studies do suffer from the problems identified above, it is difficult to dismiss the sheer consistency of the findings detailed earlier. However, the existing body of work on the EP is so limited, and attempts to measure possible changes of attitudes and behaviours have been conducted rather clumsily. A more thorough empirical investigation, that seeks to avoid the methodological problems evident in previous work, is clearly in order.

Theoretically wrong?

As indicated in Chapter 1, much of the work reviewed in the first section of this chapter has significant theoretical problems. As a body of work it is characterized by a tendency to be highly opaque about the theoretical assumptions underlying the process by which individuals are posited to become more pro-European as a result of their service in EU institutions. How does such a process work, and why? To the extent that one can deduce an (implicit) causal process within most of this literature, it appears to suggest a three-stage process:

- 1: Individual enters an institutional setting
- 2: Individual spends time in that setting
- 3: These experiences lead to changed attitudes and behaviours

However, such a causal understanding requires substantial elaboration. By itself, the above model says little or nothing about two fundamental matters:

1. *The Nature of the Experience.* Contacts and experiences in the institutional setting are meant to prompt attitudinal and/or

behavioural changes. But why? On this issue, most authors remain very unclear about *what* exactly is meant to promote the socializing effects that are assumed to be so prevalent.

2. *The Nature of the Individual.* Again, much work has been strikingly silent on this issue. Why might individuals respond to broader contextual influences in such a way as to alter their previous attitudinal and behavioural patterns? The implicit assumption usually seems to be that political actors are more or less passive receptacles who, sponge-like, 'absorb' the beliefs and attitudes of those around them. As this approach has been heavily criticized by scholars of mass politics,[28] there seems even less reason to accord it serious status as a basis for studying political elites, like those serving in EU institutions, who can be expected to be more politically sophisticated and self-conscious than mass publics. A more substantial conceptualization of these individuals as political actors within an institutional context is surely necessary.

A serious and coherent theoretical explanation of why political actors might 'go native' in EU institutions must address these two matters. Equally, any explanation of null empirical findings should also meet this criterion. These matters are therefore discussed at length in Chapter 4.

Conclusion

This chapter has, necessarily, ranged widely in reviewing previous work relevant to the concerns of this study. The assumption that individuals serving in EU institutions, including the EP, are subject to a pervasive tendency to be socialized into more 'European' attitudes, has been shown to be one that is widely held. This assumption has also been shown to have some support in thinking about institutional socialization processes across several academic disciplines. But it has also been demonstrated that little

---

[28] For instance, Dunleavy (1979: 413) has observed: 'We cannot simply assume that political alignments "brush off" on people as they walk by on the street.'

evidence has been discovered to support this assumption. In the final section of the chapter, ways of bridging the gap between theory and evidence were considered. Later chapters in the book are devoted to more detailed empirical investigation. Chapter 4 will take up the challenge indicated at the end of this one, and develop further our theoretical understanding of the issues with which the study is concerned.

4

Understanding Institutional Socialization

Chapter 3 demonstrated that, although it has often been assumed or asserted that members of EU institutions become socialized into more pro-integration attitudes and behaviours, the basis for such statements is currently weak. Little empirical evidence has been found in support of such views. Furthermore, the theoretical underpinning for these arguments remains sketchy. Although there is apparent support from studies in other disciplines and in other contexts that stress the ubiquity of institutional socialization effects, it has rarely been made explicit *why* we should expect members of the EP, or other EU bodies, to 'go native'. Upon what assumptions is this expectation based? Alternatively, on what basis might an explanation of 'null' findings—that members of institutions like the EP do not tend to become more identifiably pro-integration in their attitudes and behaviours over time—be constructed?

This chapter, therefore, leaves matters of empirical evidence aside for the moment, and addresses directly the theoretical weaknesses of previous studies. As explained in Chapter 3, any argument about institutional socialization is dependent upon assumptions about both the institutional context that is the potential socializing force, and the individuals who may be socialized. Thus, to argue that membership of the EP socializes individuals in the direction of greater pro-Europeanism, one must make certain assumptions about both the EP and about the MEPs themselves.

The discussion in this chapter is therefore structured around a critical re-evaluation of these assumptions. The first section of the chapter demonstrates that for many MEPs, their experience of 'Europe' within the Parliament is rather more ambiguous than is often suggested. The degree of 'value consensus' existing in the EP is quite limited, while MEPs' immersion in supranational politics is restrained by the fact that most remain strongly tied to national politics, and in particular to the national parties to whom they generally owe their position in the chamber. Indeed, it will be suggested that the traditional categorization of the EP as a supranational institution is in many respects quite misleading.

The second part of the chapter considers the MEPs themselves in greater detail, contrasting the typical emphasis of institutional socialization studies on how socialization facilitates individual effectiveness within the institution, with the absence of such theoretical clarity in the literature on EU institutions. After considering the potential insights of constructivist approaches, the discussion draws upon rationalist thinking to explain how the pursuit of MEPs' core political goals—(re)-election, higher office and policy—would be more likely to be hampered, rather than assisted, by them 'going native'. The concluding section of the chapter then summarizes the cumulative effect of the arguments developed, and anticipates their implications for the empirical analysis that follows in later chapters.

The institutional context: the 'Supranational' parliament?

The concept of 'supranationalism' was written into Article 9 of the Paris Treaty that established the ECSC in the early 1950s. In practice, however, there was, as Ernst Haas observed, considerable confusion as to precisely what the term, and the 'supranational jurisdiction' that the new Community apparently enjoyed, might mean in practice. Haas's own attempt (1968: 59) at a working definition concluded that supranationalism 'means the existence of governmental authorities closer to the archetype of federation than any past international organization, but not yet identical with it'.

Although not included in the Rome Treaties, the term 'supranational' has continued to be used for analytical purposes since then by scholars of the EU. In practice, however, popular usage of the word has come to mean something slightly different from the meaning imputed by Haas. Rather than connoting a distinct *type* of international governance, modern scholars of the EU have come to define and use the label 'supranational' almost exclusively to mean simply a level of governance above that of the nation state or member state. Thus, Moravcsik (1991), in using 'Supranational Institutionalism' as a variant of neofunctionalism against which to compare his 'Intergovernmental Institutionalism', refers to certain EU-level institutions (particularly the Commission) as being supranational. More recently, the work of Stone Sweet and Sandholtz (1997; Sandholtz and Stone Sweet 1998) posits an integration continuum, with one end-point being 'intergovernmental politics', and the other being 'supranational politics'. For them,

[a] 'supranational' mode of governance is one in which centralized governmental structures (those organizations constituted at the supranational level) possess jurisdiction over specific policy domains within the territory comprised by the member states.   (1997: 303; cf. Cram et al. 1999: 5)

Within this general understanding of the term, it is quite natural for those writing about the EU's institutions to regard some of them as falling naturally into the category of 'supranational', with the EC, ECJ, and EP fitting most obviously here (e.g. Cram et al. 1999: 6; Nugent 1999: 504–5). Thus, regarding the latter body, Nugent observes:

The European Parliament is supranational by virtue of being composed of directly elected Members of the European Parliament (MEPs) rather than governmental representatives, by virtue of taking its decision by majority... vote, and by virtue of having real decision-making powers.   (Nugent 1999: 137; see also Dinan 1999: 270)

All this is relatively unproblematic and uncontroversial. But following on from this initial categorization of the EP as a supranational institution, a number of further assumptions about what we might broadly term the 'institutional context' of bodies like the EP seem to have entered through, as it were, the conceptual back-door. These assumptions are difficult to tease out because of the lack of explicitness in much existing literature. But a considerable amount of writing about the EP, including much of that making some of the strongest claims about the impact of institutional socialization upon MEPs, carries within it two assumptions that are key to understanding why experience of the parliament might be expected have a strong socializing impact upon those within it.

The first assumption is that serving within an EU-level, supranational institution like the EP means to a large extent divorcing oneself from the national political scene. That is, those working for the EC or ECJ, and those elected to the EP, are expected to spend the bulk of their time in an identifiably 'European' setting, working on identifiably 'European' matters. As far as the EP specifically is concerned, this understanding suggests that service within it means largely removing oneself from the workings of national political organizations and the concerns of national politics.[1]

The second assumption is that a strong culture of shared norms and values exists in the EP that can readily be inculcated to new members. That is, in a similar manner to how other institutions with strong, shared values are able to inculcate newcomers into those values (see, for instance, Fenno's (1962) discussion of the House of Representatives' Appropriations committee, discussed below), the EP socializes new members into certain broadly shared and deeply established values and beliefs. In the case of the EP, the most prominent values to be so diffused are those of pro-Europeanism: a general favourability towards integration, with perhaps some manifestations particular to the chamber, most

---

[1] In addition to appearing in much of the textbook literature, this assumption is stated explicitly in the work of Featherstone (1979) reviewed in Chapter 2, see also Abeles (1992) and Johanssen (1995: 23).

notably strong support for greater powers for the EP itself. Thus, even when writing about the EP in the pre-direct elections era, Kerr observed that MEPs 'are exposed to a set of parliamentary traditions and norms, which place an exceedingly high value on a strong commitment to regional integration' (Kerr 1973: 71); more recently Johassen has contended that 'MEPs develop a distinct language and community, with their own codes and symbols. In so far as these are common for all MEPs they form an *"esprit de corps* or institutional solidarity"*, which, one could argue, favours "European elite formation" ' (1995: 20; see also Katz, 1999: 43).

The collective impact of these two assumptions is to conceptualize the experience of serving in the EP as one, where MEPs are exposed to a strong and sustained 'dose' of pro-Europeanism; in consequence, these individuals are under heavy pressure to absorb supranational values. However, the central claim of this section of the chapter is that both of these assumptions are in fact highly questionable. Indeed, there is good evidence to suggest that they are overstated, or even to a substantial extent simply wrong. This being the case, traditional understandings of the institutional context of the EP must also be placed into considerable doubt.

The latter of these two assumptions can actually be dealt with relatively briefly. While it is quite true that the EP has consistently supported pro-integration stances, and has indeed been a leading voice for these positions at times (Corbett 1998), it is also true that opposition to such opinions within the EP has grown steadily, the 1999 and then the 2004 elections returning to the EP its greatest ever number of Euro-sceptics. But more importantly for present purposes, the idea that there is a strong general consensus among MEPs around shared norms and values is almost certainly misplaced. A broad pro-integrationism may prevail, although this is hardly unique to the Parliament, and would be shared by most MEPs' domestic parties. But the most detailed study of political values in the EP conducted thus far found that a consensus on political values was conspicuously lacking. Indeed, the authors of this study suggested that the diversity of opinion within the EP seems so great that it is far from obvious which opinion could conceivably form the basis for a future widely adopted norm.   (Bowler and Farrell 1999: 219)

Given that MEPs represent such a broad range of political parties, nationalities and viewpoints, these findings should probably not surprise us. They do, however, cast into some doubt the idea that there are likely to be powerful, widely shared norms and values into which new European Parliamentarians could readily be inculcated.

What about the former of the two assumptions stated above: that being elected to the EP requires an individual to become a 'supranational' politician? That is, to what extent is it true that MEPs spend the bulk of their time working in a European setting and thus become substantially divorced from the concerns of national politics and the activities of their national parties? Intuitively, this appears likely to be an incomplete picture. Political scientists have long been aware of the importance for politicians of their electoral base (e.g. Fenno 1978, Mayhew 1974). Members of the EP generally attain membership of the Parliament through being nominated by, and elected as, members of national parties, within elections that are usually dominated by national parties and national issues. We could therefore plausibly expect MEPs, through political necessity if nothing else, to pay a fair degree of attention to the national political scene, and to accord a significant priority to maintaining links with their national party.

There are several ways in which we can use empirical evidence to gauge the extent to which MEPs do become divorced from the national political scene. First, we can consider how MEPs expend their time and political activity. Is it true that MEPs are generally away from their national base for prolonged periods of time, and are thus uninvolved in domestic politics? To answer this question, we can draw on information from a survey of MEPs conducted in 2000. (Further details on this survey are presented in the Appendix.) First, Table 4.1 presents some simple information regarding MEPs' political activity: do they regularly engage in political work

TABLE 4.1   MEPs' time spent on political work in home country*

Response	
Most of time each week	7.4%
Some time each week	56.3%
Limited time, mostly at weekends	33.7%
Little or no time	2.1%
N	190

*'How much time do you spend on political work in your home country rather than work at the European Parliament?'
Source: The MEP Survey 2000.

in their home country? The evidence in regard to this question is very clear: a significant majority of MEPs—more than 60 per-cent—report spending at least some of their time in every week on domestic political work; those who report spending little or no time on such matters is barely more than 2 per cent. Although the question does not, unfortunately, distinguish between different types of political work in their home countries—such as policy work for the national party or meetings with constituents and groups—the basic message of the data seems plain: most MEPs do maintain regular contacts with their domestic political base. Becoming an MEP does not mean that one ceases to be involved in political activity in one's own country.

Further evidence can be adduced by considering information from the same survey regarding the extent of contacts that MEPs have with prominent figures in national politics—national parlia-mentarians and the leadership of their domestic party. Table 4.2 presents information on this matter; once again, it shows that the vast majority of MEPs maintain very regular contact with these important national political figures. More than four-fifths have contacts with national parliamentarians on at least a monthly basis, and over 70 per cent have that degree of regular interaction with figures from the leadership of their national party.

These figures suggest strongly that most MEPs make significant efforts to ensure that they do not lose touch with national politics

TABLE 4.2   Frequency of contacts between MEPs and National Party figures*

Response	National Party leadership	National MPs
At least once a week	28.9%	28.6%
At least once a month	42.8%	53.5%
At least every 3 months	18.7%	10.8%
At least once a year	4.8%	5.4%
Less often	4.7%	1.1%
No contact	1.1%	0.5%
N	187	185

*'How frequently are you in contact with the following groups, people or institutions?'
Source: The MEP Survey 2000.

and their domestic political base.[2] Nonetheless, it remains possible that while MEPs may need to protect their political base at home, they could over time come to regard their activities in the EP as of greater importance, and even consider that the representation of views (such as ideological positions) on a European-level is of more importance than the interests of voters and their own party in their particular member state. On the latter point, Johanssen (1995: 18–9) observes that 'For most MEPs there is a strong sense of belonging to the Party Group'; moreover, the degree of voting loyalty to their multinational party group is, among most MEPs, very substantial. However, as Hix (2002a) has conclusively demonstrated, when the position of the party group conflicts with that of a national party, most MEPs will follow their national party in their voting behaviour. Furthermore, as is shown in

[2] An illustrative example of this was provided in a recent profile of the Portuguese MEP, Carlos Coelho, which observed: 'Coelho is not afraid of becoming disconnected from his electorate. After all, he goes home to Portugal on weekends, has an interactive website through which members of his constituency can put questions to him.... "Living and Working in Europe is not some kind of exile!" he says emphatically' ('Profile: The Enthusiast', The Parliament Magazine, 25 March 2002, p. 27).

TABLE 4.3 Perceived importance among MEPs of different groups represented*

Group	Of little importance				Of great importance	MEAN
	1	2	3	4	5	
All people in Europe	13.7	8.9	18.9	26.3	32.1	3.54
All in own county	3.7	6.9	19.1	34.0	36.2	3.92
National Party	4.9	11.4	24.3	33.5	25.9	3.64
EP Party group	7.0	11.4	28.6	38.4	14.6	3.42

*'How important is it to you to represent the following groups of people in the European Parliament?'
Source: The MEP Survey 2000.

Table 4.3, most MEPs do put national considerations above those of the EU as a whole. On average, most regard representing the interests of voters in their own country as more important than those of voters across the EU, and they place representing the interests of their particular national party ahead of the interests of their party group.

Furthermore, although our direct interest here is with MEPs alone, evidence from a 1996 survey allows us to compare MEPs with National Parliamentarians on some of the criteria presented in Table 4.3. On a 7-point scale (where '1' represented 'of little importance', and '7' stood for 'great importance', both types of representative were asked to state the importance given to representing their National Party, and 'all the people in' their country. Only small (and statistically non-significant) differences are found between MEPs (mean 5.46, $N = 297$) and National MPs (mean = 5.51, $N = 1,340$) for the National party item; interestingly, however, MEPs actually scored *higher* than their national counterparts in the importance given to representing the national populace (mean = 5.77, $N = 302$ for MEPs; mean = 5.52, $N = 1,345$ for national MPs; $p = 0.01$). This again reinforces the point that national considerations are not unimportant for MEPs.[3]

[3] For details of the 1996 survey, see the Appendix.

None of the evidence reviewed above should really be regarded as very surprising: as most MEPs owe their election to their national parties, it is not particularly remarkable that they continue to devote considerable time and energy to maintaining links with their domestic political base, and give their principal political loyalty to their national party. The 'electoral connection' may operate differently in European, compared to national, politics, but that does not mean that it does not operate at all (Carruba 2001, Faas 2002; Hix 2003,). When one bears in mind other ways in which MEPs' ties to their national party tend to be reinforced even when working within the parliament—for instance, the mundane but possibly quite important fact that MEPs' offices in both Brussels and Strasbourg are almost always grouped together in national party contingents (within the areas set aside for the broader ideological blocs)—the principal conclusion that one can draw from this section is that, while they do serve in an EU institution, most MEPs remain to a substantial extent *national* politicians in both their activities and their political loyalties. And it is more than reasonable to suggest that most MEPs receive a rather less full-blooded dose of 'supranationalism' when in the EP than has traditionally been assumed.[4]

A broader question, indeed, is raised by this discussion: to what extent is it actually reasonable or helpful to continue the practice of labelling the EP as a 'supranational' institution? Clearly the Parliament is not an intergovernmental body: many, indeed the majority of, MEPs do not come from parties represented in the governments of member states, and even those that do are, of course, sent on the basis of their own electoral mandate. However,

---

[4] Furthermore, we should also remember that even a relatively full-blooded 'dose' of Europe might not necessarily be viewed positively by MEPs. For many, their experience of life in the chamber could be alienating rather than inspiring. The chamber tends to be dominated by the larger party groups—and also, to some extent, by the larger national delegations. Experiencing life as a marginalized MEP within a smaller group and/or from a smaller member state might tend to make an individual less favourable towards the EU. (I am grateful to Tapio Raunio for clarifying these points to me.)

not being intergovernmental should not automatically render an EU institution 'supranational'. The EP does operate 'above' the level of national politics in terms of where and how its powers are deployed. But this is true of all EU bodies, including the resolutely intergovernmental Council of Ministers and European Council. Along with the Committee of the Regions (whose members generally hold office or have other major responsibilities at a regional level within EU member states), and the Economic and Social Committee (whose members represent significant economic and social interests within member states), the EP falls within a category of EU institutions that do not neatly fit within either 'box' created by the supranational/intergovernmental dichotomy. In the case of the Parliament, whose members are elected on a national basis, in elections generally dominated by national parties and in which national political issues predominate, and who once elected retain strong links with national politics and particularly their national party, the label *inter-national* is surely more accurate than either of the conventional alternatives. The implications of this point will be developed further in Chapter 7.

Empty vessels? Understanding European parliamentarians

The first half of this chapter explored one important dimension of institutional socialization—the nature of the experience undergone. This section identified a prime reason why MEPs might not be inclined to adjust their attitudes and behaviours in a substantially more pro-European direction: because of the absence of a strong 'value consensus' in the Parliament, and because most European Parliamentarians retain strong links to national politics, they receive a rather milder and more ambiguous dose of 'Europe' that is frequently supposed.

However, even a relatively mild stimulus in this direction could potentially have a significant impact on individuals; conversely, even strong pressures can be resisted. The impact of socialization processes ultimately depends very heavily on the individuals themselves. How will they respond to the environment surrounding them, or the messages that they receive? Given the potentially innumerable ways in which humans can interpret and react to external stimuli, any serious theory positing a uniform or at least dominant response to particular stimuli must carry within it a powerful explanation of *why* it is that individuals will respond in that way.

Unfortunately, one generally searches in vain in the existing literature on EU institutions for explicit assumptions about precisely *why* members of these bodies might respond positively to any pressures to 'go native'. Most work positing such socialization effects appears to be based on relatively simple—indeed, one might fairly say simplistic—notions of 'contact'. That is, that mere presence in a certain environment—in this instance, the EP—is supposed to lead to particular changes in individuals' perspectives—in this instance, them becoming more pro-integration. Individuals thus appear in the story as little more than 'empty vessels' into which influences of Europeanism are absorbed.

It is difficult to take this position seriously, not least because, while few social scientists doubt that individuals are shaped by their experiences and their surroundings, mere contact is not enough to guarantee particular effects. As Burbank (1997: 126–7; see also Checkel 2003: 210) has observed:

There is scant evidence to support the hypothesis of personal contact as the sole mechanism of contextual effects... [rather] social context appears to exert a reinforcing or enhancing effect on people sympathetic to the dominant party rather than a conversion effect.

The recent, constructivist-inspired, work of Checkel has attempted to specify more precisely the circumstances in which socialization (which he links to the process of argumentative persuasion) can be effective. However, it is not clear that his efforts take us much further. First, there are significant theoretical problems with the specific hypotheses that Checkel derives (see the discussion in Chapter 3, and also Moravcsik 2001). In addition, two conditions that Checkel suggests for facilitating the effectiveness of argumentative persuasion—that it will be more effective when the 'persuadee' has relatively few deeply ingrained 'Cognitive Priors', and that it will be more effective when occurring in less politicized and more insulated settings—are likely to apply only infrequently in EU institutions, and even more rarely to members of the EP—an explicitly politicized setting, most of whose members probably *will* have strong prior beliefs on major political issues, including European integration.

Thus, a coherent explanation of why members of European institutions might or might not 'go native' remains to be developed. In order to take matters further forward, the remainder of this section of the chapter will do two things. First, it will attempt to outline the lessons that major works outside the context of the EU have for understanding the circumstances in which institutional socialization processes are effective. Second, this understanding will then be applied to MEPs.

When does institutional socialization work?

There is no doubt that institutional socialization processes can, and often do, exert a powerful impact upon the attitudes and behaviours of people. As Chapter 3 noted, this is a widely supported finding across several academic disciplines. But the questions remains: Why do such socialization processes work? Or, to specify the question in a more fruitful way, *under what sorts of conditions* are individuals likely to be socialized into absorbing the prevailing values and norms of an institution?

It is difficult to generalize across the vast range of literature that examines organizational socialization in one context or another.[5] But one generalization that remains valid across many contexts is the importance of notions such as 'learning' and 'effectiveness'. Indeed, some actually define socialization in such terms—a process by which individuals 'are transformed from organizational outsiders to participating and effective members' (Feldman 1976:

---

[5] For an excellent, if now slightly dated general review, see Falcione and Wilson (1988).

309; see also Ostroff and Kozlowski 1992: 849). Much of the organizational psychology literature views socialization primarily in terms of the learning of institutional norms, learning how an organization works, and how as an individual one can be effective within it.[6] Thus, in a classic work, Louis (1980) conceptualized the process of adaptation to an organization as being about 'sense-making'. Part of this process involved developing an awareness of, and often coming to adopt, certain values that underpinned the functioning of the organization.

In a similar manner, the important recent work by the political scientist Chong (1999) has emphasized the links between socialization and rational self-interest in the development of preferences and social norms. In particular, Chong argues strongly that norms are most likely to become 'internalized' by individuals when such norms are consistent with an individual's strategic interests. Thus, there is a strong rational component to effective socialization; and hence, to understand how and when socialization occurs, we need to understand how it relates to and interacts with interests.

The relevance of this link between the process of socialization and the broader aims of an organization and the individuals within it can perhaps most clearly be illustrated, for current purposes, by reference to two classic works in modern political science. Fenno's landmark study (1962; see also Fenno 1973) of the Appropriations Committee in Congress included a powerful story about how the norms of the committee are transferred to neophyte legislators. As part of their adaptation to service on the committee, individuals came to be aware of, and generally to support, norms such as respect for seniority and a generalized scepticism about federal government spending. But why did these new committee members accept such norms? Part of the reason, Fenno (1962: 311) suggested, was the extremely strong value

---

[6] A similar understanding of socialization as the learning of established norms and behaviours underpins the recent International Relations analysis of Johnston (2001).

consensus that had become established throughout most of the committee. In addition, Fenno observed that socialization, where it occurred, reflected learning about the norms and values of the committee, reinforced by an array of rewards and punishments for individual committee members. Those accepting the committee norms would be likely to yield long-term benefits in terms of opportunities to attain positions of power (such as subcommittee chairships) and pay-offs in terms of policy outcomes; those challenging the norms would find such benefits much harder to obtain, and their political life becoming much more difficult.

In short, Fenno's study suggests that Members of Congress did not come to accept the powerful norms of the Appropriations Committee because they were brainwashed, or simply accepted what they were told. Rather, these norms became adopted and endorsed by new committee members because to do so was highly congruent with achieving their fundamental political goals— office, policy, and re-election. To state this is not to deny that attitudinal changes on the part of Members of Congress were, for the most part, genuine, or to claim that these Representatives were wholly self-serving; it does suggest, however, that socialization will be most effective when it can be linked to individuals' effectiveness in achieving their own principal goals.

A similar moral emerges from work conducted in a very different time and place: namely, Putnam's justifiably celebrated study (1993: ch. 2) of regional government in Italy. Considerable evidence is found of ideological depolarization occurring among members of Italian regional councils over the time period of Putnam's research (the early 1970s onwards). Putnam is able to trace only a small part of this ideological convergence to 'electoral replacement' of more extreme councillors; similarly, nationwide political trends are seen as being of only modest importance. Most of the change that occurs is linked to 'institutional socialization'. As Putnam suggests,

Years spent grappling together with the difficult challenges of forging a new organization taught the regional councillors the virtues of patience, practicality, and reasonableness.   (Putnam 1993: 38)

Putnam's work thus leads to similar conclusions as those generated by Fenno: socialization worked because it was *necessary* for political actors who wished to become effective in the institutional settings in which they were located. And it reinforces the essential point that serious-minded politicians do not simply absorb beliefs from 'the ether', or merely because they come into contact with people with certain views. Rather, politicians tend to be directed towards the achievement of important political goals. And to the extent that their beliefs are shaped by their experiences, then politicians' attitudes are likely to come into line with what they have found to be politically practical, with what supports the achievement of those goals.[7] We now need to consider what implications these lessons have for our understanding of MEPs.

MEPs' core political goals

If institutional socialization of political actors is most effective when it facilitates the achievement of those actors' core political goals, we need then to consider what those core goals are likely to be, and, in the specific instance of MEPs, whether 'going native' in terms of attitudinal and behavioural shifts in a more identifiably pro-European direction would actually be likely to help MEPs achieve their goals.

Most contemporary political science work, particularly that based upon broadly rationalist premises, assumes that elected

---

[7] A broadly similar, if more general, argument is made by Moravcsik in his exchange with Checkel:

> Rationalist theories...do not deny that actors in international affairs have ideas in their heads...collective ideas are like oxygen or language; it is essentially impossible for humans to function without them. They are ubiquitous and necessary tools to coordinate social life....Rationalists deny *only* that *exogenous* variation in other sources of those ideas decisively affects ideas and therefore policy...ideas are present but not causally central. They may be irrelevant and random or, more likely, they are 'transmission belts' for interests. (2001: 229, emphasis in original)

politicians strive to achieve some combination of three principal goals—Office, Policy and (Re-)Election (e.g. Hall 1987). For some (e.g. Mayhew 1974), election is seen as the primordial goal for representatives—not least because it is the minimum requirement that must be satisfied before other goals can be sought. For other authors (e.g. Strom 1990), these three overarching goals tend to be traded off against each other, with the nature of the trade offs incurred in particular circumstances being shaped both by the individual politician and by the nature of the institutional setting within which they find themselves.

The relationship between Office-, Policy-, and Election-seeking goals, and the behaviour they may induce in politicians, can be the subject of very complex theorizing and modelling.[8] But for current purposes, such efforts are largely irrelevant. More pertinent is simply to consider whether the achievement of any or all of these goals is, in the specific institutional context of the EP, likely to be facilitated in many instances by politicians adopting more pro-integration positions, or whether the adoption of such positions is essential in order to achieve policy, office, or election aims.

Office: Election to the EP does not open up (at least directly) a career path that includes the holding of executive governmental office. The EP is part of a system of 'separated' institutions in which executive power is wielded elsewhere (primarily the Commission and the Council of Ministers) rather than anything approximating a 'parliamentary' system of governance in which the executive emerges from the Parliament. However, there are a number of different positions of power and responsibility within the chamber: these include Chairships within parliamentary committees and Rapporteurships on important committee reports; leadership positions within the multinational party group and/or national party delegation; and Parliament-level positions including President, Vice-President and Quaestor. Achievement of these positions is generally acknowledged to be shaped in part by

---

[8] For an exploratory discussion of the relevance of Policy, Office and Election goals in the context of the EP, see Scully et al. (1999).

personal competence (Corbett et al. 2000); it is also driven strongly, however, by the complex system sharing out of positions across nationalities and party groups that the Parliament has developed. In addition, a number of researchers have investigated other factors that may drive the holding of office positions. Bowler and Farrell (1995) find that seniority within the chamber is only weakly related to office holding in EP committees, while Whittaker (2001) shows national political experience to be as or more beneficial to the gaining of office in the EP. And Kreppel (2002: 201–2) finds that allocation of office benefits in the Parliament is unrelated to either greater participation in the chamber or greater loyalty to the party groups. But there is no suggestion in any of this work that greater pro-European fervour is an important factor behind the gaining of office.

Office opportunities also exist outside the EP. Service in the Parliament may operate as a 'stepping stone' or as part of a political education for a future career in national politics through subsequent election to the national parliament or even the attaining of ministerial or party office positions (Scarrow 1997; Westlake 1994). But it is pretty implausible to think that this avenue of political advancement would be facilitated by individuals adopting positions on integration that were substantially more pro-integration than the mainstream in their national party. 'Going native' would be only likely to marginalize an individual within their party and thus damage their political credibility.

Policy: The EP has become, as discussed in Chapter 2, an increasingly viable and effective route through which individuals' or parties' policy objectives can be pursued. Moreover, the diffusion of power in the chamber via its committee structure appears to open up considerable opportunities for individual politicians to have a substantial impact upon policy—a common theme in interviews with MEPs (particularly from the UK) is the greater scope they enjoy to 'make a difference' over policy when compared to their national legislative counterparts. The ability of MEPs to shape policy outcomes is a function of many things: the powers of the EP in an area, the attitudes of other EU institutions and member state governments, as well as the individual representative's own abilities in advancing proposals. But to the extent that an individual MEP has the opportunity to alter policy outcomes, then expertise in the particular policy area, hard work, and the political skills needed to win support from others will all be at a premium in exploiting those opportunities; fervent pro-integrationism is essentially irrelevant.

(Re-)Election: As has been observed earlier in this study, and elsewhere (e.g. van der Eijk and Franklin 1996), MEPs are elected in polls that attract low public interest and turnouts, and in which—despite the elections being to an EU institution—national parties and national political issues predominate. Most MEPs are not themselves nationally well-known political figures; moreover, even if they were, in most countries they have little ability to affect their individual electoral fate by garnering a 'personal vote'. The majority of states in the EU conduct EP elections using either a 'closed' party list electoral system—in which voters may vote only for a party, and have no scope to favour particular candidates—or 'semi-open' systems, where there is still very limited scope for individual candidates to gain enough votes to alter their position on a party list (Farrell and Scully 2003). Thus, for most MEPs and candidates for the Parliament, their electoral fate is doubly in the hands of their party: first, they depend on the party choosing them as a candidate, and in a potentially 'winnable' position on the party list; second, to be certain of getting in they require the party to do well enough in the election itself. Fervent pro-integrationism is unlikely to help MEPs with either being re-selected as a candidate, or with winning more votes for their party. More important—particularly for being selected as a candidate—will be that they retain strong links with their national party.

Conclusion

This chapter has sought to advance our theoretical understanding of institutional socialization processes in the EP. Specifically, it has attempted to understand why widespread expectations that service in institutions like the EP should lead to attitudinal and behavioural changes in a pro-integration direction have, generally speaking, remained unsupported by empirical evidence. Although the discussion in this chapter was made more difficult by the lack of theoretical and conceptual clarity in much previous literature, some important points have nonetheless been made.

First, it has been shown that, at least as far as the EP is concerned, those serving in European institutions are likely to receive a less powerful and unambiguous dose of 'Europe' and 'Europeanism' than has often been assumed. The EP does not have a strong set of shared values to pass down to new members; moreover, while serving as MEPs, most elected representatives remain heavily involved in national politics and the work of their national parties, and they continue to regard the national political scene as highly important. To a substantial extent MEPs are, and remain, national politicians.

Second, it has been argued that it is not credible to regard political actors like European Parliamentarians as 'empty vessels' into which external influences can be fed. They are serious politicians with fundamental political goals that are likely to be similar in kind to those of other elected representatives. And they are most liable to be 'socialized' by external influences for the same reasons as others: when such socialization is part of a learning process that facilitates their achievement of fundamental needs and objectives. The achievement of most MEPs' primary goals— Policy, Office and (Re-)Election is unlikely to require, or be substantially facilitated by, a fervently pro-integration stance.

There are, therefore, good reasons to believe that the core assumptions that underpin expectations of EU institutions socializing their participants into more pro-integration attitudes and behaviours are, at least in the context of the EP and its members, highly flawed. Of course, whether a detailed empirical investigation will uncover evidence that MEPs do tend to 'go native' or not remains to be seen. This will be the task for the chapters 5 and 6 of the book.

5

Investigating MEPs' Attitudes

Chapters 5 and 6 present the main empirical analysis of the book. While Chapter 6 examines several aspects of MEPs' voting behaviour within the EP, this chapter explores more directly the political attitudes of European Parliamentarians. In line with the discussion in Chapter 4, the main concern here will be to consider the relationship between individuals' political attitudes and their experiences within the EP. Is there any evidence that service within the institution is associated with more 'pro-European' attitudes?

'Attitudes' have been defined in contemporary social psychology as being about 'passions and hates, attractions and repulsions, likes and dislikes', and to encompass 'evaluating a particular entity with some degree of favour or disfavour' (Eagly and Chaiken 1998: 269). As such, attitudes have a cognitive component—people must have at least some notion of what it is that their attitudes relate to—but they are primarily matters of emotion and evaluation (either positive or negative).[1] Of course MEPs have, as do others, innumerable attitudes concerning a potentially infinite number of objects. Our attention in this chapter will be directed to those attitudes that are pertinent to the subject matter of this study. Thus, we will consider several types of attitudes: MEPs' orientations towards European integration in

---

[1] A further important point to note is that attitudes are not generally regarded by social psychologists as being directly observable phenomena; rather, they are 'inferred from observable responses' (Eagly and Chaiken 1998: 269).

general terms, their degree of identification with Europe, and their more specific views about both the EP as an institution and the development of its powers on the one hand, and the development of European policy competences on the other. Any tendency of MEPs to 'go native' could be expected to manifest itself in greater degrees of support for integration in general, in greater identification with 'Europe', and in favourability towards the empowerment of the EU's elected Parliament and the enhancement of the EU's competences in key policy areas.

Two detailed surveys of EP members have been carried out in recent years. These provide us with a wealth of representative attitudinal data about MEPs. The first of these surveys was administered in 1996, in parallel with a similar survey of Members of National Parliaments (MNPs) in the EU (and is hereafter referred to as the MEPMNP survey). Four years later, another survey of EP members was conducted (the MEP2000 survey). Both surveys have particular strengths (discussed below), and thus data from both will be used in this chapter. The second half of the chapter draws on data from MEP2000 to explore in detail the relationship between service in the EP and members' attitudes. First, however, we look at a comparison between MEPs and their national counterparts.

European and national parliamentarians compared

This section of the chapter draws from data gathered in the 1996 survey of MEPs and the parallel surveys of MNPs in order to compare the relevant attitudes of these two types of parliamentary representatives. As indicated in previous chapters, a socialization hypothesis suggests that, *ceteris paribus*, MEPs should adopt broadly more 'pro-European' positions than their national counterparts (possibly reflecting not only the impact of socialization on MEPs, but also an equivalent process engendering more 'national' values among those serving in national institutions). The hypothesis would further suggest that differences between the two types of parliamentarians should be positively associated with the length of time individuals have spent in their respective institutions. The alternative, broadly rationalist perspective articulated in Chapter 4 would predict null findings—with limited, if any, differences between the two types of parliamentarians. However, we must also remain aware that any statistical relationships may be confused by the impact of 'selection' effects—either self-selection by those seeking to become candidates for the EP, or through the choices made by either party selectorates (over who becomes a candidate) or voters (over who finally gets elected). It may be that members of the different types of parliament have systematically different views because there are systematic differences in the types of people who put themselves forward as potential candidates, get chosen as candidates and/or get elected to the national versus European level. Thus, the analysis here must proceed cautiously and in awareness of this fact, and can contribute only a part to the cumulative 'jigsaw' of empirical evidence in this study.

The MEPMNP data is examined extensively in a volume edited by Katz and Wessels (1999), two chapters from which have direct relevance to this study. Katz (1999) explores representatives' views on their preferred 'Locus of Legitimation' for democratic politics in today's Europe (the EP or national parliaments), and their preferences over the 'Relative Influence of the EP' (compared to national parliaments). His analysis does point to some apparent differences in the expected direction between MEPs and MNPs on these measures; however, these differences are small in magnitude, and regression analysis suggests that MEPs' length of tenure in their chamber stands in a non-significant (and sometimes negative) relationship with support for a more powerful EP. Franklin and Scarrow (1999) compare MEPs and their national counterparts within regression models seeking to predict representatives' attitudes on three dependent variables: satisfaction with how democracy works in the EU; their favourability to policy decisions being made at the EU level on number of issues (which are used to form a single additive scale); and their more general favourability to integration (assessed by combining attitudes in two specific and high profile areas—a common currency and reducing national borders). They find little evidence of great differences between the two categories of representative, concluding that 'MEPs are barely more pro-European than national MPs, and certainly much less than would have been expected given many of the assertions made casually on this topic' (Franklin and Scarrow 1999: 52).

These analyses would thus appear to offer little support for the hypothesis that institutional socialization has a substantial impact on parliamentarians' attitudes to integration or EP powers.[2] Nonetheless, it is possible that greater support might be found for this hypothesis from the MEPMNP data for, while generally persuasive, the analysis of both Katz and Franklin and Scarrow is nonetheless subject to certain limitations and flaws that may conceivably account for some of their findings. A first point of concern is the dependent variables specified in the analysis. Both dependent variables deployed by Katz concern the powers of the EP *in relation to* those of national parliaments. While this makes perfect sense for addressing the particular question with which Katz is concerned (whether European or national parliamentary institutions can act as the basis for legitimation of the EU) both variables are highly problematic as broader measures of parliamentarians' attitudes to integration. Both variables, the locus of legitimation and relative influence of the EP, posit parliamentary institutions at the EU and national levels of government as zero-sum antagonists for political power. Given that many scholars believe European integration to have empowered national executives at the expense of parliaments (e.g. Moravcsik 1993, 1994), this is a difficult position to sustain; it would be entirely reasonable for parliamentarians to desire an increase in the importance of parliaments, at both national and European levels. There is certainly

---

[2] It is, therefore, all the more surprising that Katz attributes the minor differences between MEPs and MNPs in part to 'socialisation into the norms of the institutions, regardless of the respondents' prior beliefs' (Katz 1999: 43).

no *necessary* opposition between desiring greater powers for parliament at one level and the other. And nor, in practice, is one manifested in the data. Over the entire (unweighted) sample of MEPs and MNPs, the correlation between individuals' desired importance of national parliaments and of the EP (when these two are measured separately) is not significantly different from zero ($r = -0.02$, $p = 0.37$).[3]

Similarly, constraints imposed by their research design (the need to link their analysis with information gathered in the 1994 European Candidates Survey so that the attitudes of some MEPs can be measured across both surveys), forces Franklin and Scarrow to adopt rather problematic dependent variables. Interpreting their measure of 'satisfaction with democracy in the EU' is difficult: do negative responses to this question imply a belief in the nation state as a more appropriate level of political authority, or a desire to strengthen and further democratize EU institutions? The data suggests that this is a poor measure of positive attitudes towards the EU and EP: the correlation between high scores on satisfaction with democracy in the EU, and support for a more important EP (measured directly as the desired importance of the EP) is small and non-significant ($r = 0.03$, $p = 0.20$), while the relationship with support for increasing the responsibilities of the EU in general is also far from overwhelming ($r = 0.24$, $p < 0.00$). A much stronger association obtains with respondents' state of satisfaction with democracy in their own country ($r = 0.42$, $p < 0.00$).[4] In addition, as indicated above, Franklin and Scarrow's measure of representatives' generalized support for integration does not actually gauge this directly, but rather

[3] The correlation between desired parliamentary authority is negative and significant among MEPs ($r = -0.21$, $p < 0.00$), but among MNPs is actually positive ($r = 0.04$) though non-significant ($p = 0.13$).

[4] For all correlations, variables were recoded (where necessary) so that pro-EU responses score highly; non-answers were coded as missing data. As before, correlations were conducted on the full (unweighted) sample of MEPs and MNPs.

combines support for action in two specific areas (monetary union and removing national borders).

As our analysis is not restricted in the same way as that of Franklin and Scarrow, and in order to measure representatives' relevant attitudes as clearly and directly as possible, two dependent variables are specified in what follows. To gauge representatives' general attitudes towards European integration, responses are examined to the question 'Do you favour, or are you against increasing the range of responsibilities of the EU'? (answers to which were coded on a 7-point 'thermometer scale' ranging from 'very much in favour' to 'very much against').[5] Also examined are answers to a question that asked 'Can you say how much influence the following institutions and organs ought to have concerning decision-making in the EU?' with 'the EP' one of the institutions enquired about (with answers coded on an 11-point thermometer scale from 'very little influence' to 'very much influence').

As a first stage in our analysis, we simply compare the mean scores of the two types of representatives (MEPs and MNPs) on our two dependent variables. As Table 5.1a shows, the two types of parliamentarians do differ significantly on both measures, and in the expected direction each time. MEPs *are* more likely to favour enhancing the responsibilities of the EU in general, and they desire a greater level of influence within the EU for the EP. However, this simple comparison may be misleading in several respects. First, while MEPs from all fifteen member states of the EU (as of summer 1996) were surveyed, the MNP sample includes only eleven countries. This may skew the representativeness of the MNP sample—particularly as the countries omitted from the national parliaments study were Austria, Denmark, Finland, and the UK. These four include some of the most Euro-sceptical states in

---

[5] An additional advantage of using this measure is its high degree of functional equivalence to the question on integration self-placement that is used in the analysis below based on data from the MEP2000 survey.

TABLE 5.1   Average (mean) attitudes of MEPs and MNPs

TABLE 5.1A   Unweighted responses

Item	MEPs (mean)	MNPs (mean)	F-statistic
Increased responsibilities of EU	5.09	4.48	30.49 ($p < 0.001$)
Influence of EP	8.84	8.31	9.86 ($p < 0.01$)

TABLE 5.1B   Responses weighted by national population

Item	MEPs (mean)	MNPs (mean)	F-statistic
Increased responsibilities of EU	5.18	4.78	13.57($p < 0.001$)
Influence of EP	8.99	8.73	2.97 ($p = 0.09$)

the EU, with some of the most anti-EU political parties; thus, it is quite possible that the simple comparison of means between MEPs and MNPs understates prevailing attitudinal differences between the two groups of parliamentarians. A second problem with the simple comparison of MEPs and MNPs is that response rates between different countries varied substantially, and particularly so for the MNP study.[6] Both of these problems can be allowed for to a certain extent by weighting the data in order to reflect countries' relative size in the EU, which is done in Table 5.1b. Now, while MEPs still appear to be more pro-European than national parliamentarians, the differences on both variables are substantially attenuated, and become non-significant in relation to the desired influence of the EP.

However, a further problem in simply comparing MEP and MNP attitudes is that such a comparison makes no allowance for different levels of success by parties in different elections. It is

[6] The MEP study attains a relatively low Duncan index of dissimilarity (a measure of the unrepresentativeness of a sample) by country (9.11); however, differences across the MNP study are considerable, with response rates varying from 14.9 per cent for Italy to 90.3 per cent for Sweden.

widely known that EP elections tend to produce significant 'pro-test voting' and other phenomena that make them very different from national parliamentary elections (van der Eijk and Franklin 1996); once one has allowed for differences between representatives' parties, the gap between MEPs and MNPs on the dependent variables may either diminish or be enhanced.

Thus, there is a clear need to account for several potential confounding factors in comparing the attitudes of MEPs and MNPs on our two dependent variables. The best way to do this is via a simple multivariate model. First, a series of dummy variables for the nationality of each representative (the 'reference' category, for which no dummy is entered, is Austria) are included. To help account for differences between the balance of national political parties and ideologies represented in national legislatures and in the EP, three further variables are included. Data gathered by Ray (1999) that measures national parties' favourability to European integration is drawn upon.[7] In addition, a measure of representatives' placement of their national parties on the left-right ideological spectrum is included. This is entered into the model in two forms: directly, and in a form 'folded' around the mid-point of the scale, to tap into differences between centrists and extremists (with extremists scoring highest on this folded measure). And, finally, a dummy variable was included for whether an individual was an MEP (coded '1') or an MNP (coded '0'). If, once the factors measured by the other variables have been controlled for, MEPs still have more positive views on the development of integration and on enhancing the EP's role, then the coefficient for the MEP dummy variable should be positive and statistically significant.

This model was applied to the two dependent variables outlined above in an OLS regression analysis. Results are reported in Table 5.2. The fit of the models to the data is reasonable, and some important findings emerge. Several of the nationality dummies are

---

[7] Ray's work draws on expert ratings; his ratings for parties in 1996 are those used here. Missing values (where a party was not rated) are replaced by the mean for the EP party group of which the MEP was a member at the time.

TABLE 5.2   Regression estimates (*t*-statistics) for increased responsibilities of EU and desired influence of EP

Variable	EU responsibilities	EP influence
MEP	0.56 (5.15)‡	0.44 (2.57)†
Left-right placement of party	−0.11 (5.22)‡	−0.20 (6.25)‡
Left-right placement of party (folded)	0.09 (2.73)‡	0.01 (0.12)
National party position on integration	0.48 (14.83)‡	0.35 (6.70)‡
Belgian	1.58 (2.87)‡	1.49 (1.72)*
Danish	−1.02 (1.21)	−1.75 (1.38)
Finnish	−0.23 (0.33)	−0.96 (0.88)
French	0.79 (1.44)	0.23 (0.27)
German	1.03 (1.91)*	1.42 (1.66)*
Greek	0.91 (1.62)	1.75 (1.98)†
Irish	1.18 (2.10)†	−0.50 (0.56)
Italian	2.42 (4.41)‡	1.65 (1.91)*
Luxembourg	0.98 (1.64)	−0.62 (0.66)
Dutch	1.21 (2.15)†	0.94 (1.06)
Portuguese	0.85 (1.52)	−0.21 (0.23)
Spanish	1.58 (2.90)‡	1.31 (1.53
Swedish	−0.00 (0.00)	−1.04 (1.21)
British	0.65 (1.06)	0.76 (0.78)
Constant	1.02	6.66
Adjusted R^2	0.29	0.22
N	1580	1542

* $= p < 0.10$; $^{\dagger} = p < 0.05$; $^{\ddagger} = p < 0.01$

significant, with representatives from some countries generally seen as being more pro-integration indeed being associated with such stances. The party-ideological variables also have some predictive impact. Unsurprisingly, representatives from more pro-integration parties adopt such positions on our two dependent variables; once we have controlled for the ideological extremity of parties, those on the left are also more pro-integration. Our measure of extremity has a more inconsistent and puzzling impact—it has no significant relationship with representatives' views on empowering the EP, and is actually somewhat positively associated with support for increasing the responsibilities of the EU. This latter finding can be probed further; but for now, the important point is that these findings reinforce the importance of allowing for national and partisan differences in comparing the attitudes of MEPs and MNPs.

The crux of the matter, however, concerns the variable for the different types of parliamentarians: Are MEPs significantly more 'pro-European' once other factors have been accounted for? The answer is generally 'yes', but with some qualifications. On our more general measure of support for integration, MEPs are significantly more positive, although the substantive difference between them and MNPs indicated by the coefficient (just over 0.5 difference on a 7-point scale) is not very big.[8] The difference between MEPs and their national counterparts is even smaller in the case of support for greater EP influence. Here the coefficient is statistically significant, but the substantive difference this equates to (barely more than 0.4 on an 11-point scale) is minute.

While this analysis hardly gives a ringing endorsement to the idea that MEPs will have more pro-European attitudes than MNPs, there is enough suggestion of difference between the two categories of representatives to warrant investigation into whether those differences that are observable are a function of institutional socialization post-entry, rather than some form of selection effect. If the former is the case, we should expect some relationship between length of service in an institution and attitudes; if the latter is more important, greater length of exposure to the potential forces of institutional socialization should be unrelated to parliamentarians' views.

---

[8] It should be noted that specifying an alternative measure of general support for integration as the dependent variable in this model does not strengthen the relationship between membership of the EP and support for integration; if we use 'satisfaction with democracy in the EU' as our measure, the MEP coefficient fails to attain significance at the 0.05 level.

To examine this, a revised model is developed and applied to both of the dependent variables included in the previous analysis. We eliminate, from this model, the dummy variable that simply distinguishes between the two types of parliamentarians, and replace it with two variables relating to individuals' length of service in their current political institution. Unfortunately, the MEPMNP data-set records the length of service of MEPs and MNPs not in years, but only in three ordinal categories;[9] nonetheless, even this crude measure can give us some insight into whether parliamentary experience is related to representatives' attitudes.[10]

The model also includes the party-ideological variables specified in the previous analysis, and the set of nationality dummies. In addition, two further dummy variables, concerned with the impact of representatives' previous political experiences, were also included: whether or not representatives have ever been members of their national legislature (coded '1' for all MNPs and for those MEPs who have been national parliamentarians), and whether they had ever held national ministerial office. Either or both of these experiences might be posited to instill a greater attachment to national political institutions and national sovereignty.

Table 5.3 reports the results of this analysis. Overall, the relationships for individual variables are generally similar to those reported above, although the fit of the model is in both instances more modest. The most important findings, however, relate to the length of service variables. There is a significant negative relationship between MNPs' length of service in the national legislature and our second dependent variable (enhancing the influence of

---

[9] The categories are: 0–5 years service, 6–10 years, and 11+ years.

[10] The two parliamentary experience variables are specified such that members are scored '1' if they have been a member of their current institution for up to five years, '2' if a member for 6–10 years, and '3' if their experience is eleven years or greater. MEPs are then scored '0' on the national parliament service measure, and MNPs similarly score '0' on the EP service measure.

TABLE 5.3 Regression estimates (*t*-statistics) on MEPMNP data, integration and desired influence of EP, with measures of experience in Parliaments

Variable	EU responsibilities	EP influence
MEP* length of service	0.16 (1.52)	0.07 (0.46)
MNP* length of service	−0.06 (0.90)	−0.31 (3.28)‡
Left-right placement of party	−0.06 (2.52)†	−0.17 (4.81)‡
Left-right placement of party (folded)	0.07 (1.68)*	−1.72 (0.28)
National party position on integration	0.42 (9.57)‡	0.13 (2.11)†
Current or former national MP	−0.44 (2.10)†	0.25 (0.81)
Current or former national minister	0.23 (1.66)*	−0.30 (1.49)
Belgian	1.79 (2.06)†	0.22 (0.18)
Danish	−1.72 (1.18)	−5.55 (2.91)‡
Finnish	0.02 (0.02)	−2.68 (1.60)
French	0.73 (0.86)	−1.36 (1.12)
German	1.22 (1.44)	0.21 (0.17)
Greek	1.00 (1.15)	0.57 (0.46)
Irish	1.07 (1.15)	−1.58 (1.20)
Italian	2.43 (2.86)‡	−0.24 (0.20)
Luxembourg	1.10 (0.77)	−1.95 (0.96)
Dutch	1.11 (1.29)	−0.42 (0.34)
Portuguese	0.93 (1.06)	−1.66 (1.33)
Spanish	1.72 (2.02)†	0.04 (0.03)
Swedish	−0.07 (0.08)	−2.88 (2.30)†
British	0.45 (0.50)	−1.07 (0.84)
Constant	1.68	9.60
Adjusted R^2	0.22	0.18
N	1127	1112

* = $p < 0.10$; † = $p < 0.05$; ‡ = $p < 0.01$

the EP). This indicates that greater experience in a national parliament may promote an attachment to national political institutions and, conversely, engender a reluctance to empower EU-level bodies like the EP. But of greatest interest to our study is the *absence* of any significant relationship between service in the EP and representatives' support for closer European unity (on either dependent variable). Serving longer in the EP does not appear to make MEPs more favourable either to integration in general, or empowering the EP in particular. These results suggest that such—small—attitudinal differences as exist between MEPs and MNPs are most plausibly attributed to selection effects (as well as some socialization effect within *national* parliaments): they certainly give us no reason to believe that service in the EP socializes representatives into more 'pro-European' attitudes.

Probing further with alternative data

While highly interesting and quite informative, the results from the above analysis are only able to offer partial insights into the concerns of this study. In particular, it would be of interest to explore in greater detail than is possible with the MEPMNP data the potential impact of representatives' experiences in the EP on their attitudes. This data-set imposes certain important limitations on analysis, reporting as it does a limited and crude measure of representatives' experience in their respective institutions. It also offers us only limited information in relation to a crucial aspect of potential institutional socialization effects—MEPs' attitudes to the EP itself. Fortunately, however, we have an additional source of data to call on. A further survey of EP members was conducted in autumn 2000 by the EP Research Group; the following analysis is based on evidence drawn from the findings of this survey. (See Appendix for details on the MEP2000 survey, including response rates and the representativeness of the sample obtained.)

Although the MEP2000 survey returned a lower response rate for MEPs than the MEPMNP study, as a source of information it also has several advantages. Not only is the data more recent; crucially for purposes of this study, it overcomes the two specific limitations of the MEPMNP data-set mentioned above. First, it has more precise data on individuals' length of experience in the EP (measured in years), permitting a more refined test of the impact of this factor on MEPs' attitudes. Second, regarding those attitudes themselves, the survey carried a greater number of questions related to the concerns of this study. In particular, MEPs' attitudes to the EP itself were probed in some depth; there were also questions included on other aspects of potential interest, including MEPs' strength of identity with Europe, and their views on particular policy areas. Before examining responses on these questions, however, MEPs' more general orientations towards integration are considered.

To capture their broad attitudes towards the European integration process, we asked representatives 'Where would you place yourself on the question of European integration?' with responses to be placed on a 10-point 'feeling thermometer' scale whose outer points were 'European Integration has gone much too far' and 'The EU should become a federal state immediately'. Though clearly bearing a strong functional similarity to the question in the MEPMNP study on increasing the EU's range of responsibilities, this question arguably offers a slightly more direct probe of representatives' attitudes to the integration process in general. The use of the 10-point scale also offers a slightly more refined measure than the 7-point scale used in the MEPMNP measure. As Figure 5.1 shows, while MEPs' attitudes to integration are clearly skewed towards the positive end, there is nonetheless considerable variation right across the range.

Our interest here, however, is less in the absolute distribution of MEPs' attitudes towards integration, than in explaining the variation that we observe. In particular, is it possible that those who are more enthusiastic about integration are so, because of the accumulation of institutional socialization experiences? Initial indicators would suggest that this is unlikely: the bivariate correlation between MEPs' support for integration and their length of service as an MEP (in years) is, though positive, modest and not close to attaining statistical significance ($r = 0.09$, $p = 0.21$).

Nonetheless, it is entirely possible that the bivariate relationship between the two variables is influenced, and possibly weakened, by other factors. A proper test of whether MEPs' attitudes on integration are shaped by their length of service in the EP requires the construction of a multivariate model of individuals'

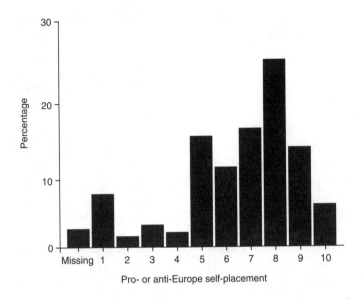

FIGURE 5.1 Distribution of MEPs along integration self-placement scale

attitudes to integration, to account for such potential countervailing factors. This is done in the analysis reported in Table 5.4. The first variable specified in this model is length of service for each MEP. In the initial specification tested below (Model 1) this measures the number of years an MEP has spent in the chamber as an elected member. However, it has often been suggested that institutional socialization processes are likely to have their most intense effects early on in an individuals' career, and thereafter to undergo progressively diminishing returns. To account for this possibility, and following the practice of previous studies (Mughan et al. 1997; Arnold 1998; Scully 1998, 2002) a second version of the model (Model 2) is specified in which the natural log of years as an MEP, instead of the linear specification, is included. Then, a direct measure of respondents' age (in years) is also included in the model. This variable allows some control for generational differences between MEPs. It could be that differences between MEPs of different longevity in the parliament are simply an artefact of broader generational differences in views; the

TABLE 5.4   Regression estimates (t-statistics) for MEPs' self-placement on integration spectrum

Variable	Model 1	Model 2
Age	−0.01 (0.67)	−0.01 (0.43)
Female	−0.74 (2.34)[†]	−0.73 (2.28)[†]
Years as MEP	0.03 (1.19)	
Years as MEP (natural log)		0.06 (0.42)
Ex-national MP	−0.95 (2.64)[‡]	−0.98 (2.74)[‡]
Ex-national minister	0.96 (2.09)[†]	0.99 (2.17)[†]
Left-right self-placement	−0.28 (3.38)[‡]	−0.29 (3.40)[‡]
Left-right self-placement (folded)	−0.01 (0.05)	−0.00 (0.01)
National party position on integration	0.62 (6.00)[‡]	0.62 (5.92)[‡]
National benefit from EU membership	1.27 (3.26)[‡]	1.29 (3.30)[‡]
EU popularity in home country	0.01 (1.35)	0.01 (1.27)
Constant	2.53	2.45
Adjusted $R2$	0.41	0.41
N	184	184

* $= p < 0.10$; † $= p < 0.05$; ‡ $= p < 0.01$

inclusion of an age variable helps control for such a possibility. A further control variable for the gender of MEPs is also included (coded '1' for female, '0' for male). Arguments have been made that female representatives differ from male counterparts in style and views (e.g. Bystydzienski 1992; Norris and Lovenduski 1996): here we can see whether at the EU level they have differing views as well.

The impact of MEPs' previous political experiences is once again assessed by two dummy variables, for whether or not a representative has ever been a member of their national legislature, and whether they have ever held national ministerial office. Partisan and ideological sources of variation in MEPs' attitudes are also considered: once again, a measure of the attitudes towards integration of MEPs' national parties is included;[11] in addition, we include two measures of members' own ideological self-placement

---

[11] This measure again draws on the data of Ray (1999), based on an assessment of party attitudes in 1996, the most recent year for which attitudes are reported.

(on a scale of 1–10, with 1 being furthest left and 10 furthest right). This variable is included in two forms—as the simple left-right spectrum, and in a form 'folded' around the mid-point of the scale. Finally, we include variables to account for broad national differences. However, unlike in the analysis of the MEPMNP data, we do not need controls for vast differences in response rates across different EU member states with the MEP2000 data. The rather unwieldy procedure of including dummy variables for each country is therefore unnecessary;[12] we instead include two variables tapping directly into reasons why MEPs from different countries might have different attitudes towards integration. These variables measure the popularity of EU membership within an MEP's country (gauged from Euro-barometer data contemporaneous with the MEP2000 survey),[13] and a question that asked MEPs directly whether they felt that their country has benefited from EU membership (coded '0' for 'not benefited', '1' for don't know and '2' for 'benefited').

Table 5.4 reports OLS regression estimates for both Models 1 and 2. Both models obtain a reasonable fit to the data, although that for the linear specification is marginally superior. The findings are substantially similar across both models, however, which indicates them to be robust. Several variables make a significant contribution to predicting MEPs' attitudes on integration: gender (with female MEPs being slightly more sceptical of integration); left-right self-placement (with greater hostility to integration being found among MEPs on the left of the political spectrum); national party positions on integration (arguably reinforcing the view that MEPs are strongly linked to their national parties); MEPs' own perceptions of their country having benefited from

[12] As a check on the results reported here, the model was rerun with the national dummy variables included. No substantial differences obtained with regard to the variables of greatest interest to our study from the results reported in the main text.

[13] This measure is taken from Euro-barometer fifty-four (fieldwork conducted in Autumn 2000, the closest Euro-barometer survey to the time when the MEP2000 survey was conducted); the measure specified here is the net (% 'good thing' – % 'bad thing') evaluation by citizens of their country's EU membership.

EU membership (which, quite unsurprisingly, is positively associated with support for integration); and prior political experience
(with former ministerial experience, slightly surprisingly, associated with being marginally more pro-integration, but former national parliamentarians being distinctly more sceptical). The
other variables are not significantly related to the dependent
variable.

Of greatest interest, however, is the fact that MEPs' length of
service in the chamber has no observable impact on their integrationist stance. The coefficient for both specifications of this variable is at least positive, but experience in the EP does not come
even remotely close to attaining statistical significance as a predictor of MEPs' attitudes on integration.[14]

Our general 'feeling thermometer' measure of attitudes towards
closer European integration, of course, by itself offers only a rather
crude insight into MEPs' political attitudes. Indeed, it is possible
that it may not capture the most important consequences of a
process of institutional socialization, which may be less in the
direction of general support for 'integration', and more related
to changed attitudes in specific areas. A particularly strong possibility is that institutional socialization may build an attachment
to the institution itself: that MEPs come to be increasingly supportive of an enhanced role in the EU for the EP (Shepherd 1996).
Fortunately, the data from the MEP2000 survey give us considerable scope for testing such a possibility.

A number of attitudinal items related to the role of the parliament within the EU were included in the survey. As shown in
Table 5.5, there is considerable attitudinal variation to be
explained. That these items are not merely more specific

---

[14] It must be noted that this finding is emphatically not an artefact of the specific
model specification used here. Alternative specifications—including, for instance,
replacing the two 'national difference' variables used here with a set of nationality
dummies—fails to produce any consistent relationship between experience in the
EP (either in the linear or logged form) and attitudes to integration. Details available
from author.

TABLE 5.5 MEPs' opinions (%) on the powers of the EP

Item	Strongly agree	Agree	Neither agree nor disagree	Disagree	Strongly disagree
The EP should have more power to influence interest rates under EMU	6.0	18.5	12.0	28.3	35.3
Justice and Home Affairs policies should be adopted using the co-decision procedure	26.6	47.4	8.3	12.0	5.7
The EP should have the power to reject some foreign policy decisions under CFSP	18.3	50.8	7.9	15.7	7.3
The EP should have the right to initiate legislation	33.3	44.1	5.1	12.3	5.1
The EP should have equal powers with the Council in all areas of lawmaking	34.0	37.7	4.2	18.3	5.8
The EP should be able to amend all areas of expenditure in the EU budget	36.6	48.5	5.7	7.7	1.5
The commission president should be nominated by the EP, rather than national governments	31.3	36.5	10.4	17.2	4.7
Commissioners should be individually approved by the EP under the assent procedure	30.2	41.7	11.5	14.6	2.1
The EP should be able to remove individual commissioners from office	30.9	41.2	8.2	14.9	4.6

manifestations of a general orientation towards integration is shown by simple correlation coefficients between the integration 'feeling thermometer' scores and the different items: most of the correlations are below 0.5, and some are even non-significant. However, collectively these nine items generate a highly reliable Likert scale of MEPs' opinions on the position of the EP within the institutional structures of the EU.[15] An additive scale based on MEPs' responses to the nine questions has therefore been constructed, in order to gauge representatives' strength of support for a strong role for the EP within EU.[16]

The simple bivariate correlation ($r = -0.08$; $p = 0.32$) between MEP's scores on this scale and their length of service (in years) as an MEP again does not attain statistical significance. Moreover, this time the coefficient is actually negative: contrary to a socialization hypothesis, it suggests that MEPs become, if anything, *less* likely to support greater EP powers the longer they spend in the institution. The multivariate analysis reported in Table 5.6 replicates Models 1 and 2 from Table 5.4, but with the EP powers scale as the dependent variable this time, rather than MEPs' integration self-placement scores. A third version of the model is also specified (Model 3) which includes MEPs' attitudes on the general integration item (and specifies MEPs' length of service in the EP in the linear form).

Table 5.6 presents OLS regression estimates. Both Models 1 and 2 obtain a much poorer fit to the data than when applied to the integration self-placement scale, although this time the fit of the logged specification of the model is slightly better. Once more, however, the substantive implications of both models are largely consistent. None of the variables entered attains statistical

---

[15] The Cronbach's Alpha coefficient of reliability for the 9-item scale is 0.85. (A general rule is that items form a reasonable additive scale if the Alpha coefficient exceeds 0.7—see Pennings et al., 1999: 96–8.)

[16] Responses were recoded so that the most 'pro-EP' positions scored '5' for all items, and the least pro-EP position scored '1'. The additive scale thus runs from 9 to 45.

TABLE 5.6 Regression estimates (t-statistics) for support for greater EP powers

Variable	Model 1	Model 2	Model 3
Age	0.09 (1.37)	0.09 (1.39)	0.11 (1.96)*
Female	−1.42 (1.06)	−1.38 (1.04)	0.47 (0.39)
Years as MEP	−0.12 (1.04)		−0.18 (1.76)*
Years as MEP (natural log)		−0.66 (1.24)	
Ex-national MP	−1.79 (1.26)	−1.82 (1.29)	0.73 (0.56)
Ex-national minister	−1.27 (0.68)	−1.34 (0.72)	−3.31 (1.99)[†]
Left-right self-placement	−0.42 (1.30)	−0.44 (1.35)	0.16 (0.55)
Left-right self-placement (folded)	−0.75 (1.31)	−0.72 (1.25)	−0.81 (1.63)
National party position on integration	0.28 (0.70)	0.28 (0.72)	−0.86 (2.24)[†]
National benefit from EU membership	1.80 (1.15)	1.75 (1.12)	−0.36 (0.25)
EU popularity in home country	0.03 (1.25)	0.03 (1.27)	0.01 (0.61)
MEPs' self placement on integration			1.86 (6.87)[‡]
Constant	28.84	28.91	23.42
Adjusted R^2	0.06	0.06	0.28
N	159	159	159

* = $p < 0.10$; [†] = $p < 0.05$; [‡] = $p < 0.01$

significance in either Model 1 or 2; and the length of service variable has a negative although non-significant, coefficient in both specifications, indicating no substantial relationship between service in the EP and attitudes to empowering the chamber. Model 3 unsurprisingly increases our ability to explain variance in MEPs' support for greater powers for the Parliament. Although most coefficient signs remain the same, in a few instances (such as age, which is now modestly and positively significantly associated with greater support for empowering the EP, and prior national ministerial experience, which now has a significant negative coefficient) variables, which had previously been non-significant now assume a stronger relationship with the dependent variable. Unsurprisingly, MEPs' general favourability towards integration is a strong predictor of their support for a more powerful EP; although once this factor is accounted for, greater enthusiasm for integration among national parties appears (somewhat counter-intuitively) to be negatively related to MEPs' support for greater EP powers.

Most importantly, however, in Model 3 the linear specification of years as an MEP also achieves a modest level of statistical significance. Yet, once again, this variable produces a negative coefficient. In other words, once the factors that this model controls for are taken into account, greater experience in the chamber is actually associated with *lower* levels of support, rather than higher ones, for enhancing the powers of the EP! We can certainly find no indication here that greater service in the EP, and thus a more sustained exposure to the apparent forces of institutional socialization, engenders in members of the institution an enhanced degree of support for empowering that institution.[17] If anything, the opposite appears to be the case.

The above findings indicate strongly that MEPs do not tend to 'go native' in the manner widely hypothesized. The posited effects of institutional socialization do not manifest themselves on measures that tap precisely the areas where such effects would most plausibly be expected. Yet it is still conceivable that there are socialization effects that have not been captured by the variables considered thus far. MEPs' experience in the EP might conceivably have a stronger and more discernible impact in other directions. Perhaps socialization shapes the extent to which representatives develop an identity with 'Europe'? Or maybe it influences the more policy-specific attitudes that representatives take towards

---

[17] Once again, these findings are definitely not an artefact of model specification. Numerous alternative specifications have failed to produce a significant positive link between service in the EP (however specified) and MEPs' attitudes on the powers of their institution. In most specifications, the coefficient for length of service in the EP is negative.

the role that the EU in important policy areas?[18] Again, the MEP2000 data provides measures that allow for these possibilities to be tested.

To assess any possible identity effects, we can look at responses to a question enquiring directly 'Do you identify most with Europe, your member state or your region?' and asking MEPs to rank these from 1 to 3. Our measure codes those who indicated a primary identification with Europe (51 of 188 MEPs answering this question) coded '3', those placing Europe second (72 respondents) coded '2', and those identifying least with Europe (65 MEPs) coded '1'. The simple correlation between this measure and the linear measure of experience in the EP is positive, but modest and does not approach statistical significance ($r = 0.11$; $p = 0.15$). The question of whether socialization might shape MEPs' policy attitudes is explored via two measures tapping into their support for the enhancement of EU policy competences. The first comprises responses to a question about the European role in foreign policy (agreement with the statement that 'the EU rather than NATO should be responsible for Europe's defence') with responses on the 5-point scale coded from '5' for strongly agree through to '1' for 'strongly disagree'. The correlation between this variable and length of service in the parliament is actually negative, and non-significant ($r = -0.06$; $p = 0.38$). In addition, an additive measure was constructed that combines responses to a series of questions as to whether the EU should acquire greater regulative power in a wide variety of policy areas.[19] Combining seven items, all of which were measured on a 5 point scale (from those desiring 'a lot more' regulation to those wishing 'a lot less') yields an additive index running from '7' (for any respondents wanting the minimal

---

[18] I am grateful to an anonymous reader of the manuscript for suggesting these further possible manifestations of a 'going native' process.

[19] The questions specifically asked respondents 'Do you think there should be more or less EU-wide regulation in the following areas?'; the areas asked about were: health and safety at work, labour rights, consumer protection standards, environmental protection standards, food safety standards, taxation rates, and on the media, broadcasting, and audiovisual standards.

regulation in all areas, to '35' (for those supporting substantially more EU regulatory capacity in all seven policy spheres).[20] This scale is, again, actually negatively (although non-significantly) correlated with the linear measure of length of service in the EP ($r = -0.04$; $p = 0.63$).

These three measures (strength of European identity, and support for expanded EU competences in both foreign policy and regulation) were then included as dependent variables in OLS multivariate regression analyses, with explanatory variables specified as per Model 1 in Table 5.6.[21] Findings from this analysis are reported in Table 5.7. While the fit of the model, and the impact of the other explanatory variables included, varies for the three different dependent variables, one thing is very clear from the analysis. There is no substantial relationship between our measure of experience in the EP on the one hand, and representatives' strength of identity with Europe, or support for extending the policy competences of the EU, on the other. Once again, observable implications of a socialization hypothesis have been tested, and they have failed to find empirical support.

Conclusion

This chapter has conducted a detailed analysis of survey data relating to the attitudes of MEPs. It has focused, in particular, on analysing their views in several areas central to the concerns of this study: their views on European integration in general; their more specific attitudes towards the role within the EU of the EP; their strength of identification with 'Europe'; and their views on the development of EU policy competences. The analysis has used alternative sources of data to consider these various observable

---

[20] The policy index forms a highly reliable scale, with a Cronbach's Alpha coefficient of 0.88.

[21] As a further test, the non-linear version of the model—equivalent to Model 2 in Table 5.6—was also run for all three dependent variables; however, this failed to produce any significantly different findings.

TABLE 5.7   Regression estimates (*t*-statistics) for identity and EU policy competence measures

Variable	Euro Identity	CFSP	Regulation
Age	0.00 (.21)	0.01 (1.20)	0.03 (.84)
Female	−0.02 (.12)	−0.09 (.39)	−1.66 (2.07)[†]
Years as MEP	0.01 (.87)	−0.03 (1.34)	−0.08 (1.18)
Ex-national MP	−0.35 (2.35)	−0.31 (1.16)	−0.22 (.25)
Ex-national minister	0.39 (2.04)	0.18 (.54)	−0.03 (.02)
Left-right self-placement	−0.06 (1.63)	−0.10 (1.62)	−1.38 (6.46)[‡]
Left-right self-placement (folded)	−0.07 (1.10)	−0.14 (1.36)	−0.42 (1.16)
National party position on integration	0.04 (1.00)	0.14 (1.84)*	0.47 (1.82)*
National benefit from EU membership	0.09 (.57)	0.24 (.82)	1.15 (1.21)
EU popularity in home country	0.01 (1.97)*	0.01 (1.80)*	0.05 (2.76)[†]
Constant	1.76	2.11	26.64
Adjusted R^2	0.09	0.09	0.40
N	179	176	173

* = $p < 0.10$; [†] = $p < 0.05$; [‡] = $p < 0.01$

implications of an 'institutional socialization' hypothesis. That a variety of tests, drawing on alternative sources of data, and examining different dependent variables, tend to lead to similar conclusions substantially enhances the degree of confidence that we can place in those conclusions. The findings thus can clearly not be dismissed as merely an artefact of peculiarities relating to a particular data-set, a specific question or one particular way of testing a hypothesis. They are robust across data sources and alternative measures.

The analysis in this chapter has offered no support to the idea that experience in the EP socializes members into more 'pro-European' attitudes. There is little evidence that MEPs are substantially more pro-integration than their national counterparts; those minor differences that do exist, appear unrelated to MEPs' length

of service in the EP; and the favourability of MEPs towards integration in general, towards enhancing the powers of the EP in
particular, towards empowering the EU further in important policy domains, or towards a sense of identification with Europe is
entirely unrelated to their length of experience in the parliament.
At the level of measurable attitudes, and to the extent that we can
assess the potential impact of socialization processes using the
cross-sectional data of surveys, our institutional socialization hypothesis is therefore decisively rejected. Rather, the findings are
consistent with the rationalist perspective advanced in Chapter 4.
Whether similar findings obtain when MEPs' behaviour is examined—rather than measures of attitudes—is the question addressed in Chapter 6.

6

Evidence from Voting Behaviour

Chapter 5 examined the potential impact of institutional socialization on the political attitudes of MEPs. The evidence suggested
that socialization processes in the EP do not have the impact
commonly attributed to them: leading individuals serving within
the institution to become more pro-integration over time. MEPs
are very marginally more inclined to favour advances in integration than their counterparts in national parliaments. However,
there is no indication that these small differences are caused by
institutional socialization among MEPs. Rather, the evidence suggested that a combination of 'selection' effects and socialization
effects among *national* parliamentarians might have shaped attitudes. But such effects, if present, are small. For the most part,
MEPs, in their attitudes on integration in general, and even in
their attitudes toward empowering their own institution, look
markedly similar to members of national parliaments. When the
views of MEPs were examined in more depth, drawing on a different data source, there was no sign of socialization processes having a systematic impact on members' attitudes. Those who have
had greater exposure to the supposedly socializing influence of
service in the EP do not have significantly different attitudes on
integration than do their less-experienced colleagues.

This chapter moves on from the analysis of survey evidence on
MEPs' attitudes towards an examination of data on MEPs' behaviour. There are two main reasons for doing this. The first is that, as
suggested in Chapter 1, it is good social scientific practice to explore

our hypotheses across as many observable implications and types of evidence as possible. Our confidence in findings is boosted if they are supported by different types of evidence drawn from a variety of sources. A second reason, however, is that while surveys do offer us detailed and quite subtle evidence on individuals' attitudes, there are also potential problems with such evidence. What politicians say is one thing; what they actually do may be rather different, and the relationship between attitudes and behaviours is by no means necessarily tautological (Searing 1994: 380). At the very least, it is entirely possible that the evidence from the 'hard' data of real, consequential political behaviour may present a different picture from that gleaned from attitudinal surveys.

The most commonly used evidence of the behaviour of parliamentarians is analysis of voting records in the chamber. As Mezey (1993: 342) notes, 'The casting of a vote is clearly behavioural, and clearly important behaviour because a defining feature of legislatures is that they make decisions through a voting process.' This chapter examines in two distinct ways data gathered from MEPs' behaviour in parliamentary votes. The second half of the chapter examines the behaviour of new MEPs over the opening months of a five-year parliament. This section uses time series data to consider whether new MEPs become more 'European' in the cues that they follow in their voting behaviour. Before that, however, attention will be turned to some of the most important individual votes occurring in the Parliament.

Evidence from key parliamentary votes

MEPs can be, and are, given the opportunity to cast votes in the EP plenary sessions on a huge variety of matters. Many votes will be on things where the EP's legislative powers can be deployed to some effect; but a large number of other votes are not. Some votes will be on matters of widespread political controversy; but many concern far more low-key issues. Some will excite interest from across the political and geographical spectrum represented in the chamber; other votes are of deep concern only to a few particular individuals, and on occasion are subject to quite low levels of participation.

The votes to be examined here were not, in any sense, 'typical' votes in the EP.[1] The analysis in this section of this chapter is based around three major votes held in the EP between 1990 and 2000. These were key divisions, where members were asked to endorse calls for closer integration and the granting of greater powers for the EP. Thus, examination of MEPs' behaviour on these votes provides for a quite different test of the potential impact of institutional socialization processes on individuals than that conducted in the previous section. While vaguely pro-integration and pro-EP attitudes might be held by members at any stage of their career, the analysis here gauges what MEPs do when they are asked to take a clear, public position. Is their likelihood of supporting closer European integration and an enhanced role for the EP in such a public and definitive manner influenced by spending some time in the Parliament, and thereby being socialized into supporting such values?

Some previous work (Scully 1998, 2002) has examined a number of important votes in the EP and found little evidence to support a socialization hypothesis. However, this work examined votes over only a limited time period (1990–6) and with a less-developed statistical model than that specified here.[2] It is quite possible, therefore, that some evidence might yet be found of a link between MEPs' service in the EP and their willingness to support closer integration in their voting behaviour in the chamber.

The votes to be examined each occurred in the period preceding the conclusion of an IGC that was negotiating revisions to the founding treaties of the EU. The final treaty texts were expected to be important in shaping both, the future of the EU in general and

---

[1] For efforts to calculate more 'typical' influences across all votes held in the EP, see Raunio (1997), and Hix (2002).

[2] Specifically, this previous examination of some key votes on integration did not include any measures of the popularity of the EU in the MEP's country, or a measure of national party attitudes towards integration.

the role of institutions like the EP in particular. Though formally excluded from the ultimate decisions at the conference—any final treaty was to be signed by representatives of national governments alone—the EP had ample opportunity to attempt to shape the agenda. Moreover (as was discussed briefly in Chapter 2), there is some evidence that over the past two decades, the cumulative effect of pressure from the Parliament has been considerable: the vast bulk of the highly ambitious programme of reforms that the Parliament set out in the early 1980s had, by the turn of the century, been incorporated into the treaties (Corbett 1998).

The three votes examined here occurred before the Maastricht, Amsterdam and Nice treaties that were the culmination of their respective IGCs. The parliamentary divisions occurred on the reports to be submitted by the EP to the IGC. All the reports were approved by the Parliament, but with some significant opposition in each case. The first vote examined (held in November 1990, during the latter part of the IGC that culminated in the Maastricht Treaty) sought MEPs' support for the third 'Martin Report', produced by the Parliament's Institutional Affairs committee (and largely authored by the British Labour MEP David Martin), which proposed a considerable enhancement in the powers of the EP among a series of proposals for EU reform. In particular, this report presented a clear proposal for the form and extent of co-decision legislative powers that many in the EP wanted. The second vote (held in December 1995) was on a resolution related to the Bourlanges/Martin report, again coming from the Institutional Affairs Committee, for a forthcoming IGC that culminated in the June 1997 Amsterdam Treaty. The resolution included demands for greater powers for the EP, notably a strengthening and extension of the co-decision prerogative that Maastricht had granted the EP as well as other institutional reforms of the EU. The final vote considered (held in April 2000) endorsed an amended version of the Dimitrakopoulos/Leinen report, and set out the EP's position before the build-up to the Nice Treaty. Though perhaps less ambitious than in previous times, the amended version of the report still saw the EP calling for a deepening of integration, including an enhancement of its own position with regard to legislative powers. (See Table 6.1 for details on the three votes.)

Each vote occurred within eighteen months of the previous EP election: it seems likely, therefore, that those newly elected at that poll should not have been too far advanced into their parliamentary career by the time of the votes examined for any process of institutional socialization to be completed. We can, thus, probe for differences in behaviours between a sizeable body of relatively new MEPs, and the many others with more substantial degrees of experience in the chamber.

For the purposes of multivariate analysis on each vote, the dependent variable in the analysis was coded '2' if an MEP supported the resolution, '0' if they voted against, and '1' if the member was present in the chamber and registered an abstention.[3] Separate OLS regression analyses were conducted for each

TABLE 6.1   Description of major EP votes analysed

Date	Description of vote	Yes	No	Abstained
22 November 1990	'Resolution on the Intergovernmental Conferences in the context of the EP's Strategy for EU'	163	22	19
14 December 1995	'Resolution on preparation of the meeting of the European Council'	346	33	45
13 April 2000	'Resolution on the Dimitrakopoulos/ Leinen report'	238	147	73

[3] Voting 'abstained' on a division in the EP is thus distinct from simply being absent from a vote. Because of the diversity of reasons that might explain a member's absence from the chamber, absent members have been excluded from the following analysis.

vote.[4] The explanatory model used for the analysis of the attitudinal data in Chapter 5 was applied in an amended form here. The model required amendment because, unlike with the survey-based analysis, direct measures of all MEPs' ideological positions, or of their own feelings about whether their country has benefited from EU membership, were lacking. Other indicators that may, albeit roughly, tap into the same factors, have therefore been substituted for both of these variables. Data on the left-right position of each MEP's national party (based on expert ratings), has therefore been included in place of direct measures of an individual MEP's self-placement on the left-right spectrum.[5] Euro-barometer data has also been drawn upon—in each instance from the survey whose fieldwork was conducted in the time period closest to each vote examined here—to present the net (positive minus negative) percentage figure for whether the public in each MEPs' member state believed that their country had benefited from EU membership. Finally, a variable indicating whether an MEP's national party was in government at the time of each vote has been included. Previous work has indicated that the

----

[4] The use of OLS regression is this instance could be questioned, given that the categories of the dependent variable essentially form an ordinal rather than an interval level scale. However, highly similar results were obtained using the Ordered Logit technique (see Scully 1998, 2002). We can therefore be reasonably confident that the results obtained here are not an artefact of the particular methods used.

[5] In the analysis here, we again draw on the ratings reported by Ray (1999) on national parties positions on integration, entering the rating gathered for the time point closest to each vote analysed. Thus, for the November 1990 vote, we report data for national party positions in 1992; for both the December 1995 and April 2000 votes, we report data for party positions in 1996. As with the analysis in Chapter 4, missing values (where a party was not rated) have been replaced by the mean for the EP party group of which the MEP was a member at the time. For left-right ratings, we draw on the data of other expert ratings. For the votes in 1990 and 1995, we use data reported in Huber and Inglehart (1995), that was gathered in 1993 except for Greece in the 1990 analysis where, due to missing data in Huber and Inglehart, we use the figures reported by Laver and Hunt (1992). For the 2000 vote we use the more recent ratings of Lubbers (2000).

presence of an MEP's party in the Council summit meetings inclines an MEP to be less supportive of an independent line for the Parliament (Hix and Lord 1996; Scully 1998).

Table 6.2 presents regression estimates for each of the three votes examined. In a similar manner to the analysis conducted for the survey data, two versions of the model were run for each vote, with the 'years as MEP' variable specified directly (Model 1) and in a logged form (Model 2). The models obtain a highly satisfactory fit for each vote, and the results are generally quite consistent across the three votes. Several aspects of the findings are of interest. Consistently the strongest single factor predicting MEPs' behaviour is the position of their national parties on integration, and in the predictable direction: quite unsurprisingly, those MEPs from more 'pro-European' parties are strongly inclined to support calls for closer integration in their voting behaviour. Other variables have a substantial impact, and in the direction that would be broadly expected. The variables for prior national political experience (as an MP or Minister) have a generally negative relationship (and often significantly so) with support for closer integration. And the coefficient for the position on the left-right spectrum of an MEPs' national party is always negative, indicating greater opposition to closer European unity being manifested on the left than the right.

Other aspects of the findings are less consistent. Support for closer integration is greater among MEPs from countries where EU membership is more popular, with the coefficients being highly significant in the two more recent votes. However, the relationship between MEPs' behaviour and public perceptions of their country having benefited from EU membership generally run in the contrary direction: the latter reflecting above all the consistent support for integration from MEPs from states like Germany, where public attitudes have increasingly focused on the costs of EU membership. The relationship between MEPs' voting behaviour and two other variables—whether or not their national party was in government, and the 'folded' measure of that party's left-right position—is also inconsistent, something

TABLE 6.2 Regression estimates (standard errors) for MEPs' behaviour in three votes

Variable	22 November 1990		14 December 1995		13 April 2000	
Years as MEP	0.03 (.01)‡		0.00 (.01)		0.01 (01)	
Log of years as MEP		0.01 (.02)		0.00 (.01)		0.02 (0.03)
Female	−0.05 (.08)	−0.07 (.08)	−0.01 (0.05)	−0.01 (0.05)	0.15 (0.07)†	0.15 (0.07)†
Age	−0.00 (.00)	0.00 (.00)	−0.00 (0.00)	−0.00 (0.00)	0.00 (0.00)	0.01 (0.00)
Ex-National MP	−0.27 (.08)‡	−0.25 (.08)‡	−0.04 (0.05)	−0.05 (0.05)	−0.09 (0.08)	−0.09 (0.08)
Ex-National Minister	0.09 (.13)	0.01 (.13)	−0.10 (0.07)	−0.11 (0.07)	−0.28 (0.12)†	−0.29 (0.12)†
Left-Right stance of national party	−0.34 (.19)*	−0.31 (.19)	−0.47 (0.10)‡	−0.47 (0.10)‡	−0.02 (0.17)	−0.02 (0.18)
Left-Right stance (folded)	0.36 (.48)	0.19 (.49)	−1.59 (0.26)‡	−1.61 (0.26)‡	1.72 (0.49)‡	1.67 (0.50)‡
National party position on integration	0.32 (.04)‡	0.31 (.04)‡	0.21 (0.02)‡	0.21 (0.02)‡	0.34 (0.03)‡	0.34 (0.03)‡
National benefit from EU membership	−0.01 (.00)‡	−0.01 (.00)‡	−0.00 (0.00)	−0.00 (0.00)	−0.02 (0.00)‡	−0.03 (0.00)‡
EU popularity in MEPs' country	0.01 (.01)	0.00 (.01)	0.01 (0.00)‡	0.01 (0.00)‡	0.04 (0.00)‡	0.04 (0.00)‡
Constant	0.03 (.37)	0.18 (.38)	1.04 (0.17)	1.04 (0.17)	−2.02 (0.30)	−2.03 (0.30)
Adjusted R²	0.47	0.45	0.45	0.44	0.45	0.45
N	204	204	415	415	455	455

$* = p < 0.10$; $† = p < 0.05$; $‡ = p < 0.01$

that may reflect differences in the specific political context surrounding each vote.

However, perhaps the most striking finding, and for current purposes certainly the most important one, is that relating to the variables measuring service as an MEP. Although the coefficients for these variables are always positive (suggesting at least some correlation between length of service in the EP and greater support for integration), on only one out of six occasions—the linear specification for the vote in November 1990—is the variable a significant predictor of MEPs' behaviour. In all other instances, consistent with the findings of the analysis of survey data in Chapter 5, and whether specified in a linear or in a logged form, this variable has no substantive impact on MEPs' likelihood to support a pro-integrationist and pro-parliament position.

Therefore, analysis of these key votes in the Parliament leads to an essentially identical conclusion as was drawn from the analysis of survey data on MEPs' attitudes. Contrary to the implication of a 'going native' hypothesis, individuals do not become more 'Europeanist' in their political behaviour as a result of service in the EP. When they have been asked to take a public stand on votes concerned with the advancement of European integration in general, and the powers of their own institution in particular, more long-serving MEPs have not been notably more likely to vote in favour of closer integration and an empowering of their own institution. In this important respect, then, the behaviour of European Parliamentarians doe not appear to be shaped by the forces of institutional socialization. Moreover, our confidence in this conclusion is strengthened by the fact that it is a finding that is robust across different votes, held at different times, and in quite different political contexts.

Adjusting to Europe? New MEPs and party voting

The empirical analysis reported in this second section of the chapter operates on a rather different basis from that conducted hitherto. So far, the analysis has been based on data that compares

MEPs with their national counterparts and/or uses cross-sectional data gathered at a single point in time. The analysis has sought to control for a number of variables—including age and party attachments—that may introduce 'cohort' effects into the data. In addition, the analysis has deliberately been conducted to use different types and sources of data, gathered at different times. All of this should strengthen our confidence in the findings of the empirical analysis thus far, particularly as those findings are so consistent.

Nonetheless, the fact that the previous analysis has not been conducted on time series data does impose some limits on the findings. To be precise, while the results are *highly consistent with* the absence of a general pattern of change in MEPs' attitudes and behaviours in a more pro-integration direction, the results are not able to show this directly. And it is thus at least conceivable that there are forms or patterns of institutional socialization that has eluded the data that has been examined so far. For instance, it may be that socialization is a very rapid process: that for many new members of the EP, the shock of entering the multinational parliamentary institutions promotes an attitudinal and behavioural change that is very rapid in nature. This possibility is, indeed, pointed to by Franklin and Scarrow (1999: 57) who contend that any—modest—socializing effects of EP membership are likely to be 'effects that occur very quickly upon entry into that body'.

If Franklin and Scarrow's suggestion were to be correct, certain methodological implications follow. Rather than socialization effects being manifest as a slow accretion (something implied in the linear specification of the empirical analyses of attitudes and voting behaviours) or as intense at first but then slowly tailing off (as implied by the logged specification), what one might observe would instead be more in the nature of a 'step-level' change of moderate degree. It is not clear that there are good theoretical reasons why one should necessarily expect socialization processes to be of this form. For instance, if socialization follows from argumentative persuasion and the expansion of cognitive horizons, then one might expect socialization effects to persist, albeit with gradually reducing intensity. Nonetheless, it remains an empirical possibility that there are undetected socialization processes going on that the attitudinal and behavioural data presented hitherto, gathered some time into five-year parliamentary terms, is not picking up.

The second section of this chapter will therefore be devoted explicitly to examining the first months of a parliamentary term in the EP. Time series data on new MEPs will be deployed to examine whether, during the months when they first come into contact with the practices and procedures of the chamber, they start to behave in a more clearly 'European' manner.

Conducting this analysis does, however, raise a problem of data availability. There are not enough number of votes in the EP on clearly integration-related matters to examine them month by month. However, this problem also suggests an opportunity to test an alternative observable implication of the institutional socialization hypothesis. In addition to shaping voting behaviour on divisions that are directly related to the integration project, a greater 'Euro-mindedness' might be manifest in terms of the orientation of an MEP to political parties. As described earlier in this study, MEPs are—with few exceptions—elected as, and largely because of, their membership of established national political parties. Within the Parliament, they are (assuming their party has been sufficiently successful to return more than one MEP) part of a national party contingent that is also, in the vast majority of instances, then part of a wider multinational party group.

For the purposes of the current analysis, it is not necessary to go into any great detail about the interaction between the major party groups in the EP, or indeed the relationship between national party cohorts within party groups: this issue has been addressed more than adequately elsewhere.[6] The more basic point that is of immediate interest is simply that, as members of both a national party and a European party group within the EP, MEPs

---

[6] For analysis of the party groups within the EP, see Raunio (2000) and Hix et al. (2003).

have to some degree a dual partisan identification. For most of the time and for most purposes, these two identities are complementary and not competitive: MEPs benefit in terms of things like committee and rapporteurship assignments, and access to staffing resources, from their national party cohort being within a large and influential party group. And when votes occur in the Parliament, most of the time national party cohorts are able to follow the broader party group line with few problems—not surprisingly, as they share a broad ideological affinity with each other, and are involved collectively in discussions within the party group in establishing the group position.

Sometimes, however, the unity of the party group breaks down, and one or more national contingent breaks ranks. A classic instance of this was the vote held in the EP in July 1994 on the nomination of Jacques Santer to be the next President of the EC. The nomination of the Christian Democrat Santer was opposed very strongly by the Socialist group in the EP, and most Socialist MEPs therefore voted against Santer. However, there was a strong counter-pressure among Socialist MEPs whose own national party was in government—meaning that their national party had therefore been involved in the European Council Summit meeting that nominated Santer. Under pressure (or in a few cases direct instruction) from their national party HQs, the majority of Socialist MEPs from this latter group of national parties backed Santer, ensuring the success of his nomination (Hix and Lord 1996).

The Santer case illustrates starkly the general point that for MEPs, their national and European partisan loyalties may come into conflict. In such situations, an MEP may have to choose between supporting their national counterparts or those in their broader ideological family. Previous work has shown conclusively that the most common response of MEPs is to side with the national party (Hix 2002). Nonetheless, while this may be the most common response, it may not be equally common for MEPs at all stages in their career. It may be that national ties are of overwhelming strength to start with, but that as MEPs become used to life within the broader party groups, the latter also become the subject of some degree of identification by parliamentarians.[7] This raises an interesting possibility for empirical analysis: among new MEPs, does one see any tendency over the opening months of the parliamentary session, as they adjust to life in the chamber, that where national party cohort and party group come into conflict, they become more inclined to vote with their 'European' partisan colleagues against the majority of their national counterparts?

To examine this, the analysis here draws on data gathered on the first six months of the 1999–2004 EP.[8] This data-set reports the behaviour of all MEPs who participated in the 246 roll-call votes held in the Parliament during this period. Every individual vote cast by each MEP counts as a single case within the data-set, which therefore contains an extremely large number of cases (93,683). For each case, a number of variables are coded, including whether the individual vote cast was different from the general party group line, and whether it differed from the line taken by that MEP's national party cohort.

As is discussed in more detail by Hix (2002), for an MEP to 'defect' from the line of the party group is rare; for them to vote against the position of the majority in their national party delegation is even less common. Among the entire universe of 93,683 votes cast by MEPs in the six-month period covered by the data examined here, only 12.1 per cent of them saw an MEP voting in the opposite direction from the majority of their party group, and a mere 3.6 per cent of votes saw defection from the line of the national party contingent.

However, it is the behaviour of new MEPs that is of particular interest here: those who were first elected to the Parliament in July

---

[7] It should be noted that attitudinal data from the MEP2000 survey do not tend to support this contention. The simple correlations between length of time served in the Parliament (years as an MEP) and degree of identification with the Party Group (measured on a 5-point scale, with 1 meaning 'of little importance' and 5 'of great importance') is actually negative although the coefficient is non-significant ($r = -0.08$; $p = 0.30$).

[8] I am grateful to Simon Hix for supplying the data used in the analysis here.

1999. Among these neophyte members of the EP, is there any observable indication of a 'step change' in their behaviour in these potentially crucial first months? Specifically, on those occasions when the positions of the European party group and the national party cohort cannot be reconciled, can one observe any indication of new MEPs beginning to develop an identification with their European partisan orientation that might lead them to defect from the position of their national party? Is there any evidence that a rapid, early socialization process that leads to MEPs moving from an initial very strong inclination to vote with the national party, to a position where siding with their European partisan colleagues becomes somewhat more probable?

To test this hypothesis, new MEPs were selected from the broader data-set—with those who were returning members from the previous Parliament, or who had been MEPs at some previous time and now returned in 1999, thus excluded from the analysis. Because of the very large proportion of new MEPs elected in the 1999 elections, however, this still left a total of 46,429 cases (votes by individual MEPs) available for analysis. The fact that there is behaviour of a substantial number of individuals across a large number of votes to examine here is helpful, because it obviates the possibility that results may be skewed by one or two untypical votes on particular issues. A variable was then generated which was coded '1' if an individual MEP's vote was in opposition to the line of their national party contingent but in support of the position of their party group, and '0' otherwise. The month in which each vote took place was then also coded (from '1' in first month of votes up to '6' in final month examined).

The empirical analysis that then follows is simple and straightforward. The percentage of votes cast by new MEPs that were defections against the national party line but supportive of the European party group position was calculated. These figures are reported in Table 6.3. The results need little sophisticated statistical analysis because the pattern—or rather lack thereof—in them is self-evident. As is shown in Table 6.3, for an MEP to vote with their European party group against their national party is a rare

TABLE 6.3 Voting defection by MEPs against national party line but for party group position, by month

Month	%
July	1.0
September	0.5
October	0.8
November	0.7
December	0.7
N of = 46,089	

event. Moreover, as a simple examination of the figures indicates, it is not an occurrence that becomes more likely over the opening months of the Parliament. Indeed, if there is any trend at all in these figures, it is actually for defection from the national party cohort and towards the European party group to become slightly *less* common: a simple linear regression using month of vote as the explanatory variable and our measure of defection as the dependent variable actually produces a negative (although, despite the large number of cases, non-significant) coefficient ($B = -0.00$; $p = 0.26$).

Thus, the evidence from this section of the chapter produces a conclusion that is very much consistent with that in the previous section, and indeed with that in Chapter 5 as well. One plausible observable implication of an institutional socialization hypothesis has been examined here: whether there is a tendency for new MEPs to manifest a rapid socialization into a greater 'Euro-mindedness' in their first months within the chamber by becoming somewhat more inclined to vote with their European party group colleagues against the majority in their national party group. The empirical evidence has provided no grounds at all to support the hypothesis. As with their more experienced colleagues, new MEPs tend strongly to vote with their colleagues from their national party. Most of the time, that also places them in accord with those in the party group. But where national and European party ties conflict, both new and experienced MEPs tend to accord priority to the national party, and this does not change for new MEPs as they adjust to life in the chamber.

One of the implications of the findings of this section is, of course, to further strengthen the argument made in the first section of Chapter 4. That is, the evidence reinforces the case that while operating for significant periods of time in a multi-national institutional context—of which the party groups are an important part—MEPs nonetheless remain to a substantial degree national politicians in their activities and outlook. This applies as much to their voting behaviour in the Parliament as elsewhere.

Conclusion

This chapter has analysed two forms of data on the voting behaviour of European parliamentarians, to consider whether there is any evidence that, in line with a 'going native' hypothesis, MEPs become over time more inclined to behave in an identifiably 'Euro-minded' or pro-integration manner. The analysis has looked in detail at behaviour on key integration votes in the chamber, and also at the behaviour of new MEPs over the first months of a new parliamentary term. The findings from these very different types of investigation are consistent in terms of their implications, and furthermore are also consistent with those of the work on attitudinal survey data reported in Chapter 5. No consistent evidence has been found to support an institutional socialization hypothesis. MEPs do not become more inclined to support measures of closer integration in parliamentary votes the longer they are exposed to the putative forces of socialization in the EP; and new MEPs show no increased tendency rapidly to begin voting more with their European party colleagues than their national ones on occasions when the two come into conflict.

That the findings of this chapter are consistent both with each other and with the empirical evidence of Chapter 5 raises substantially our confidence in them. That the findings so strongly contradict many widespread assumptions regarding the influence of socialization process in EU institutions, including the EP, requires also that we give serious thought as to their broader implications. Discussing these implications is the task for Chapter 7 of the book.

7

Conclusion—Becoming Europeans?

This concluding chapter of the book has three tasks: first, to summarize the arguments and findings of the study thus far, second, to discuss some potential counter-arguments against the findings presented here, and in doing so make clear some of the arguments that this study is *not* advancing, and third, to elaborate upon the implications of the arguments and findings that the book has presented. Three sets of implications will be considered: for the EP as an institution; for the study of EU institutions more broadly; and for the study of institutional socialization processes in general.

A brief synopsis

The starting point for this study was the observation that assumptions and/or assertions regarding the ability of the EU institutions to promote fundamental changes in the attitudes and behaviours of those who serve in them are both widely prevalent and highly important. And yet it was further observed that such assumptions and assertions have generally not been coherently theorized; nor have they been subjected to serious and systematic empirical scrutiny. The task established for this book was to address directly the theoretical and empirical inadequacies of our existing knowledge through a detailed study of the MEPs. The EP offered an appealing focus for the research in this study partly because of its own growing importance as an institution within the EU, partly for pragmatic reasons of data availability, but also because it seemed to offer a context where institutional socialization effects might be particularly likely to be observed.

As was shown in some detail in Chapter 3, many academic authors and other observers have argued that those serving in EU bodies, including the EP, are subject to a pervasive tendency to become more pro-integration in their beliefs and their actions. However, the limited body of previous empirical research has revealed very little support for such arguments. Furthermore, institutional socialization hypotheses have not been grounded in a coherent theoretical framework that explains why political actors like MEPs should be expected to 'go native'.

In Chapter 4 it was argued that a serious theoretical account of a process of institutional socialization requires at least two elements: a specification of the main features of the socializing experience; and an account of how and why individuals are expected to react to that external stimulus in certain particular ways. The chapter then went on to argue, first, that service in the EP gives the majority of its members a far more limited and ambiguous dose of 'Europe' than is frequently implied. Most MEPs retain substantial contacts with and involvement in national politics. Second, it was argued that it is far from clear that we should expect European parliamentarians to be amenable to 'going native'. The most highly developed literatures on the subject of institutional socialization emphasize strongly that institutional socialization is most effective when it directly facilitates an actor's effectiveness within a particular institutional context. But there is little reason to think that achieving the general goals towards which most MEPs will likely be focused—policy, office, and re-election—will be more effectively facilitated by adjusting their attitudes and behaviours in a substantially more pro-integration direction.

Finally, in Chapters 5 and 6, a variety of empirical tests on several different sources of evidence have been conducted to examine whether there is, in fact, substantial evidence that service in the EP does influence its members to become in some or other sense more 'Euro-minded' or pro-integration. The consistency of the empirical results is striking. They suggest:

- MEPs' views on integration in general, and the empowering of the EP in particular, are little different from the views of their counterparts in the national parliaments of EU member states. There is no evidence that MEPs are socialized into becoming substantially more Euro-minded than national-level representatives. Where differences between the two types of parliamentarians exist they are of very small magnitude; and they are most plausibly attributable to selection effects and to socialization processes within *national* parliaments.

- When MEPs' attitudes on integration are studied in more depth, and on a more recent set of survey data, no relationship was observed between length of service in the EP and individuals' views. Longer-serving MEPs, who have had greater exposure to the supposedly socializing forces within the EP, are no more favourable to integration than are their less 'socialized' colleagues. Nor do they support the empowerment of their institution more strongly; or identify to a greater extent with 'Europe'; or evince greater enthusiasm for expansion of the EU's policy competences.

- On key votes in the EP, when MEPs are asked to take a public position on the advancement of integration, there is no consistent relationship between service in the chamber and voting behaviour. More 'socialized' EP members are not more likely to vote in favour of advances in integration than are their less experienced colleagues.

- Finally, when the behaviour of new MEPs over the first months of a parliamentary term is examined, there is no observable tendency for them to become more likely, over time, to support their European party group over the national party on those occasions when the two take opposing positions in votes in the Parliament. There is no 'step change' in loyalty towards the European party group.

In short, the evidence presented in this study indicates that while many may have assumed that there is a pervasive tendency for actors in EU institutions to become more pro-integration, there is no substantial support for this hypothesis among one highly important group of such actors, namely MEPs. MEPs do not tend to 'go native' in the manner commonly assumed or asserted; moreover, as was argued in Chapter 4, there are very good reasons why this does not occur. Most of the rest of this concluding chapter will be devoted to considering the wider implications of the findings of this study. First, however, some potential objections and counter-arguments to the case made thus far will be considered.

Pre-empting some counter-arguments

The arguments advanced in this book are, doubtless, open not only to extension and elaboration, but also to counter-arguments. They may also be subject to some misinterpretation—for instance, by being interpreted as making larger claims than they actually are—which might in turn generate additional counter-arguments. While it would be unrealistic to attempt to consider all possible contrary views, or anticipate all the ways in which the arguments here might be misunderstood, some potential objections to the conclusions that this study draws can be identified. This section, therefore, will briefly discuss three of the more important possible criticisms of the arguments advanced here.

Has the study used appropriate evidence?

All empirical research in the social sciences (and, indeed, elsewhere) depends on evidence, or 'data', that is almost invariably limited, partial and subject to numerous imperfections. The responsibility of the scholar in this situation is twofold: to garner as much information as possible out of the evidence available; but also to avoid the temptation to claim more than can reasonably be supported by the evidence available to them.

None of the evidence used in this study is perfect. As was pointed out at various places in previous chapters, it is subject to several limitations. It is far from self-evident exactly how the key dependent variable of this study—the 'Europeanization' of individuals—should be defined. It is also very difficult to gather time series evidence pertinent to assessing the dependent variable. The approach taken here has been to draw on a variety of sources and types of data; to specify clearly what should be plausible observable implications of key hypotheses; and to conduct tests on the data in as clear and replicable a manner as possible. While each individual type of data used, and test conducted, certainly has limitations, the empirical findings should be viewed cumulatively. And the degree of empirical triangulation—the consistency of the results obtained from alternative tests conducted on different data sources—obtained is impressive, thereby raising our confidence in the results. In short, while the evidence used in this study undoubtedly *is* imperfect, it seems distinctly unlikely that the findings presented are due simply to peculiarities in that evidence or imperfections in the manner that it has been analysed.

Has the notion of 'Institutional Socialization' in the EU been conclusively disproven?

No. It is important not to overstate or overinterpret the findings of this study, and to be clear as to what can reasonably be claimed from those findings. This study has failed to find evidence to support the idea that *one particular form* of institutional socialization effect occurs within the EP. These findings should not thereby be interpreted to mean that service within the EP has no impact upon members of the institution. Socialization is a multifaceted phenomenon: all MEPs must presumably undergo very important learning experiences during their time within the Parliament. The vast majority of new MEPs doubtless face an extremely steep learning curve in finding out about the Parliament's procedures, the issues before the chamber, and the personalities and political preferences of their fellow parliamentarians. Depending on their own previous experiences and individual personalities, different MEPs will presumably react and adjust in different ways;

nonetheless, it remains highly plausible that there may be general tendencies for MEPs to adjust aspects of their attitudes and behaviour patterns during their time as elected representatives. For instance, most will learn more about how to interact with politicians from other countries and discover the sort of compromises with others that are politically necessary to advance some desired objectives. Those who do not learn these lessons, or learn them poorly, will be likely to achieve very little in the chamber. As one broadly Euro-sceptical (now retired) British Conservative MEP very bluntly expressed it, 'You get nowhere by isolating yourself in the European Parliament.'[1]

However, recognizing that much learning and adjustment will be necessary for most MEPs is rather different from making blanket assumptions that such adjustments will necessarily include major shifts, in a particular direction, in political actors' loyalties, attitudes and behaviours. An important part of the research agenda on the EP should now be to investigate how—and why— MEPs' political preferences and ways of operating may be shaped by their experiences in the chamber. This research can be more precisely directed if it is unencumbered by the notion that such experiences promote dramatic changes in a pro-integration direction, as too many previous authors have unwisely assumed.

Similarly, the findings of this study should not be taken to have decisively falsified institutional socialization as a potential influence on the attitudes and behaviours of actors in other EU bodies. It is possible that in some institutions there is a tendency for individuals to 'go native'—although the important research of Hooghe (discussed in Chapter 3) casts severe doubt as to whether this occurs to any great extent within the EC. But the discussion in Chapter 4 has provided a framework that should help scholars understand whether such institutionally induced transformations are likely to occur. This framework identifies two dimensions that need to be explored in order to judge whether and in what socialization processes are likely to be effective: first, we need to under-

---

[1] Interview, 26 March 1998.

stand in some detail the institutional context within which political actors will be working; second, and even more importantly, we need to understand the major goals that incumbents of positions within those bodies will likely be seeking.

What implications does this study have for social constructivism?

This study has gone a long way towards falsifying a hypothesis that—as discussed in the earlier chapters of the book—has been advanced over the years by many authors, a few of whom have drawn on the general intellectual tradition of social constructivism in developing their ideas. But the study should not thereby be taken as in any serious sense falsifying (or trying to falsify) social constructivism *tout court*. Broad intellectual schools such as social constructivism (or others such as rationalism or Marxism), are never simply right and rarely if ever just wrong.

Social constructivism is grounded in some important insights about the nature of social existence (e.g. Berger and Luckmann 1967); scholars across many areas of the social science have found this perspective to be of value in developing their thinking. But just as one can acknowledge that important insights have stemmed from Marxist or rationalist premises while simultaneously being aware that many Marxist or rationalist scholars have ended up pursuing intellectual blind alleys, it should be clear that one can also accept that social constructivist premises are valuable for many scholars without committing oneself to endorsing uncritically all ideas and hypotheses propounded by self-identified 'social constructivists'.[2] It is quite conceivable that a coherent theoretical position, building from social constructivist premises, might be developed to incorporate the empirical findings presented here. The wider question of the likely fruitfulness of social constructivism as the basis for studying the EU,

---

[2] Indeed, there have been studies in some areas of scholarship, pointing to instances where specific developments of social constructivism appear to be highly misconceived (see, e.g., in the field of Science Studies, Gross and Levitt, 1998).

undoubtedly an interesting and important question, goes well beyond any inferences that can reasonably be drawn from the evidence presented in this book;[3] the implications of the findings here for constructivist ideas about the specific process of European integration are considered below.

So what? The implications

The European Parliament and its members

As discussed in Chapter 1, the EP has in recent years become an increasingly important part of the institutional structures of the EU, and it is therefore more important now than ever that scholars develop their knowledge of the chamber. While much of this book has developed an essentially negative argument—demonstrating what the Parliament is *not*, in terms of the impact of service in the

---

[3] To state this does not mean that I have no views on the value of social construct-ivism to the study of the EU. The recent overview by Risse (2004) provides not only an excellent introduction to the area, but also suggests a number of areas in which constructivist insights may be particularly important. Risse thereby outlines a po-tentially fruitful research agenda. Hitherto, applications of social constructivism to the EU have suffered from a number of problems, including: a lack of clarity and precision in some basic statements of the perspective (e.g. Christiansen et al. 1999); a lack of specificity and falsifiability in the truth claims advanced (Moravcsik 2001); and a tendency to present relatively unoriginal ideas in the terminology of social constructivism as new insights (e.g. Glarbo 1999). But all of these problems are, in principle, resolvable, and do not suggest any *fundamental* reasons why social con-structivist insights may not contribute much to understanding much about the EU. This is not to deny that other hypotheses that have their inspiration in social constructivist theoretical insights will fail to win empirical support. It is almost certain that this will happen. But in such situations, it is to be hoped that social constructivists do not follow the tendency of some rationalists to treat their para-digm in a quasi-theological manner, as a position to be defended against all contrary evidence, and thus tend to ignore negative findings or to concoct ad hoc ways to 'explain them away' (see Green and Shapiro 1994; Friedman 1996). Rather, it is to be hoped that serious attempts will be made to consider the reasons for the negative findings, and their theoretical implications. The world has recently witnessed some of the drawbacks of 'faith-based intelligence policy'; faith-based social science has little more to commend it.

institution on its membership—such an argument should also carry some positive implications. So what has this study told us about the EP and about those who serve within it? At least two significant points need to be made.

The first important implication of this study for the EP arises out of addressing a question that is immediately raised by the major empirical findings of this study. That question is, 'if socialization processes do not account for the strongly pro-integration position that has typically been characteristic of the EP, then what does?' This is an important and entirely reasonable query to raise. The answer is also important in terms of its implications for the EP. It is not, however, a particularly original answer: rather, it is very similar to that offered by those (such as Ernst Haas and Henry Kerr) who conducted the first studies of the EP in the years before direct elections. Put simply, if we wish to understand why most members of the EP have been strongly pro-integration, the explanation lies, not in what happens to MEPs after they enter the Parliament, but on what occurs beforehand.

A significant part of this story in the past was probably—as Kerr's work on the non-elected EP found was the case—the selection of more pro-European individuals to serve in the chamber. And such selection effects may plausibly have continued into the elected era, whether operating through the mechanism of self-selection with disproportionate numbers of more pro-integration individuals offering themselves as candidates, or at a later stage in the choice of representatives (through pro-integrationists being more likely to be selected as candidates, and/or more likely to get elected). However, the evidence of the first half of Chapter 5 indicates strongly that even if selection effects have been manifest in the past, they are largely insignificant now: MEPs' views on integration are virtually indistinguishable from their counterparts in national parliaments. Nor should we be surprised that European Parliamentarians have very similar views on integration as national parliamentarians, because both groups emerge (for the most part) out of the same parties.

If neither selection effects nor socialization processes substantially shape MEPs' views on European integration, why then is the EP still generally a pro-integration institution? The answer, surely, lies with national politics and national political parties. The majority of mainstream politicians and political parties in the EU are, and have been, supportive of the general process of European integration. Throughout the existence of the EP, since its humble origins as the ECSC Common Assembly, being pro-integration has not been something strange, requiring an elaborate explanation. To the contrary, it has been hostility to the integration project that has been the more unusual position for mainstream European politicians to take. Thus, in Taggart's astute and evocative phrase (1998), it is Euro-scepticism that has typically been a 'Touchstone of Dissent', largely confined to the political fringes. MEPs are generally pro-integration for the same reasons that national MPs are: they are members, and representatives, of parties for whom such views are part of accepted, mainstream political opinion.

An additional and important implication of this argument for the EP then follows. As Euro-scepticism of various shades has grown in popularity in recent years (Taggart and Szczerbiak 2004) and in particular as the electoral success of Euro-sceptical forces in EP elections has increased, anti-integration figures have come to be present within the EP itself in greater numbers. This can be seen, to give but one illustration, in the voting behaviour analysis reported in the first half of Chapter 6. Opposition to the pro-integration stance adopted by the Parliament was confined to a tiny minority in 1990; by the time, ten years later, that MEPs were voting on the Parliament's position over the negotiations that culminated in the Nice Treaty, anti-integration opinion within the chamber comprised a much more substantial chunk of those voting. And were such political forces to continue to enjoy greater success in elections to the chamber, it is by no means inconceivable—if still politically somewhat unlikely—that they could at some point come to enjoy a majority position within the chamber. The strongly pro-integration position generally adopted by the EP could well, in time, come to be seen not as something inevitable and unchanging, constantly reinforced by the socialization of new MEPs into these beliefs, but as the highly conditional consequence of essentially domestic political factors.

Implications for the study of the EU

As was suggested in Chapter 1 of the book, this study has some important implications for how we understand the EU. Two such implications will be developed here—concerning how scholars approach the study of EU institutions such as the EP, and also regarding the explanation of the broad process of European integration.

The point made immediately above, namely the importance of national parties in shaping the balance of integrationist opinion within the EP, returns us to an argument that was first made in Chapter 4. It was observed there that MEPs remain, in both their activities and attachments, to a substantial extent *national* politicians; and it was further contended that the EP is generally best understood not as a supranational institution, operating above and largely divorced from the concerns of national politics, but as one dominated by the interactions of nationally based politicians.

This point is of considerable potential importance for how scholars approach the study of the EP, and indeed for how they understand the EP's involvement within the broader political processes of the EU. The basic assumptions that scholars make about political processes can do much to shape how we understand them, and the starting point for much writing and thinking about the EU is that the EP is one of several supranational institutions (along with the Commission and Court) that can be counterposed to the resolutely intergovernmental Council of Ministers. This is not merely the standard working assumption of most EU textbooks;[4] it also finds its way into the core assumptions

---

[4] For typical example (in otherwise excellent introductory texts), see Nugent (1999) and Dinan (1999); though for a refreshing exception see Hix (2005).

made by much of the research literature, such as that which has attempted to construct abstract models of the EU's main legislative procedures.[5] Thus, this latter body of work tends to assume that the key players are national governments and the supranational institutions (the latter of whom can further be assumed to be generally more pro-integration than most governments). However, it is far from clear that this is the only, or even in many circumstances the most appropriate, way in which to characterize and explore institutional politics in the EU. As a highly experienced former UK MEP observed:

There are really three sorts of conflicts in the parliament. There are the *inter-institutional* conflicts—Parliament against the Council, Parliament against the Commission—there are *party political* conflicts, which is Christian Democrats against the Socialists and so on, and then there are the *national* conflicts. . . . I spent four years as chief whip there, and part of my job when issues came up was to assess which one of these three conflicts was going to have the most powerful effect on the way people voted.[6]

The tendency in much of the EU literature to think of EU politics as operating primarily along inter-institutional lines means that we have yet to develop our ideas sufficiently about how politics in the EU may operate in a trans-institutional manner in terms of international conflicts (these, when considered, have tended to be examined only in the Council); or in terms of interparty or inter-ideological conflicts. Thinking of the EP as an important political arena where all of these conflicts are evident is likely to be more fruitful than thinking of it as a supranational institution separated from the concerns of national politics.

A second important implication of this study that was suggested in Chapter 1 concerned how we understand the broad process of integration to operate. Much recent work, notably that drawing much of its inspiration from the broader constructivist literature,

---

[5] For an excellent recent overview and further development of this work, see Garrett and Tsebelis (2000), 'Legislative Politics in the European Union', *European Union Politics*, 1: 9–36.

[6] Interview, 11 November 1998.

stands in a longer line of thinking that has viewed an important element of European integration as being about the fundamental transformation of identities and interests. This process has often been expected to operate most dramatically in the altered loyalties, attitudes and behaviours of those serving within EU institutions. But the findings of this study have at least partially disconfirmed the mechanism of institutional socialization as a means by which European integration is advanced. Specifically, we have found no evidence that such processes work in the hypothesized manner in the EP—despite the fact that, as was discussed in the opening chapters, there appeared good initial reasons for thinking that such processes should be particularly effective in the EP. And the most detailed study of officials within the EC (Hooghe 2001) has come to an essentially similar conclusion.

The manner in which the existence and development of the EU may affect countries and individuals' perceptions of Europe, and of themselves, and their identities and preferences, is an extremely complex subject. The evidence presented here constitutes only a small part of the picture, and studying these matters is an enormous, multifaceted scholarly task. In approaching this task, drawing on ideas from broader intellectual schools, such as social constructivism, that have proven themselves of value in some other areas of study, may well prove to be of assistance—by suggesting to scholars new questions to ask, new concepts through which to frame their analysis, or by enabling them to ground their hypotheses in more general understandings of the social world. And yet, as Pollack (1998:45) observes, 'Constructivist scholars of the European Union are, after all, making extraordinary claims about the constitutive effect of EU norms to literally remake EU member states and their preferences.' These claims cannot be rendered immune from the hard graft of empirical investigation and the rigorous testing of truth claims. No amount of theoretical ingenuity allows us to impose assertion or assumption where there should be evidence. Thus far, much of the best evidence that scholars have been able to uncover and analyse has yielded conclusions unfavourable to the constructivists more 'extraordinary' claims.

Studying institutional socialization

The concluding point of this study is directed most specifically at the literature on institutional socialization in the EU, but is also of relevance to other literatures where the socialization of political actors is regarded as an important phenomenon. As was observed in Chapter 3, much work that has made claims about how the identities and interests of people may be altered by their experiences has had extraordinarily little to say about the political actors who are expected to be so transformed. Whether the power of socialization processes is attributed simply to just 'being there' in a given institutional context, or is conceived in more subtle terms such as 'argumentative persuasion', those who are thereby influenced often occupy a marginal place in the discussion. Political actors appear, as was noted previously, as little more than 'empty vessels', into which certain experiences are 'poured'.

Work that proceeds on such a basis is thereby grounded—one suspects, generally unwittingly—on an extraordinarily limited view of human beings in general, and political actors in particular. All of the explanatory power is attributed to the structural context; political agents apparently just respond (more or less readily) to such external stimuli. Much work on the EU, and indeed elsewhere, that prides itself on the breadth of its ontology thereby ends up implicitly incorporating into an important aspect of its theorizing a very narrow 'stimulus-response' notion of social change. It is ironic indeed that so much work should, when positing processes of institutional socialization in the EU, have ended up echoing so strongly the 'Behaviourist' school of psychology, exemplified in the work of Skinner (1957), which was (in)famous for its highly limited conception of human mental processes and for placing an almost total emphasis on human behaviour as learned responses to outside stimuli.

The fate of Behaviourism is highly instructive. After a period of considerable intellectual popularity in the 1940s and 1950s, Behaviourism was largely blown out of the water in the early 1960s by a number of scholars who not only noted the inadequacy of Behaviourism's explanations of many aspects of human existence—such as the processes by which young people acquire and come to use natural languages—but who also advanced a more rounded ontological basis for the understanding of humanity and society.[7] Humans are not empty vessels into which experience is poured, but beings with important, innately specified capabilities. These capabilities include not only things like the ability to acquire and use language, but also creativity and self-reflectiveness. Human beings thus do not simply respond to external stimuli; they also have the ability to think about their situations, define their goals and priorities, and pursue things that they value. Thus, the influence of any external stimuli will be strongly conditioned by the nature of the human actors receiving and responding to such forces.

In many areas, social constructivist work has been entirely consistent with these insights; indeed, in applications to International Relations theory, constructivists have been among those most prominently advancing such points—contending that, for instance, anarchy in international politics does not operate like some inevitable law that defines the nature of the international system, but is 'what states make of it' (Wendt 1992). However, in the study of EU institutions, rationalist perspectives, which have often been justifiably criticized for being grounded in a highly limited ontology, are actually—as was articulated in Chapter 4—able to put forward an understanding of these institutions and how they shape those who serve within them that is ontologically broader, more realistic and more empirically accurate than any perspective that has yet been developed by social constructivists and their theoretical allies. We cannot understand

[7] For general introductory discussions of these issues, see McGilvray (1999) or Pinker (1995).

whether and how political actors will be shaped by the institutional contexts where they operate without a serious and realistic conceptualization of those actors themselves. These agents matter, as well as the structures that they serve within. This is true for EU institutions, and just as true elsewhere.

Appendix: Principal Data Sources Used in the Book

Interviews

The interview responses reported in detail in Chapter 2, and also used in places elsewhere in the book, derive from a series of eighty-six in-depth interviews conducted with MEPs and some ex-MEPs between 1998 and 1999, covering the period leading up to and the months following the 1999 election to the EP. Interviews were conducted in Brussels, Strasbourg, and—in the case of many of the interviews with British politicians—in a variety of locations throughout the UK. Sixty-five of the interviews were conducted by the author; the remainder were conducted by Prof. David Farrell, Dr Richard Whitaker, Dr Nicholas Startin, and Dr Matthew Walker. Their assistance with scheduling, conducting and transcribing interviews is gratefully acknowledged. This research received financial support from Brunel University and the Nuffield Foundation.

Interviews were conducted in English and French, and averaged almost exactly forty minutes in length. Among topics covered were individuals' reasons for seeking candidature to the parliament; the process of becoming a candidate; individuals' political priorities within the parliament; whether they perceived any tendency for either themselves or others to have their political outlook and attitudes shaped by their experiences within the chamber—and if so, how and why; and (where relevant) their reasons for leaving the parliament.

While the sample of MEPs interviewed was significantly biased towards British politicians, MEPs representing a variety of nations, parties, and levels of experience within the EP were interviewed. Table A.1 summarizes information about the interviewees.

The MEPMNP Survey

The MEPMNP data analysed in this book was produced as part of the broader European Representation Study. The 1996 surveys of MEPs and MNPs were coordinated by Jacques Thomassen and Bernhard Wessels. Fieldwork for the MEP study was conducted in May–June 1996, with the survey returning 314 responses, a return rate of 50.2 per cent. Members of elevan national parliaments in EU member states were surveyed between April 1996 and July 1997, with an average return rate of 37.6 per cent obtained among this population. For further details regarding this survey and the data-set produced, see Katz and Wessels (1999).

The MEP2000 Survey

The MEP2000 Survey was co-authored by Simon Hix and Roger Scully, on behalf of the European Parliament Research Group, and funded by a grant to Simon Hix under the 'One Europe or Several?' research programme of the Economic and Social Research Council (Grant: L213252019).

TABLE A.1

Nationality	Gender	Party group*	MEP at the time of interview?
57 British	69 Male	41 Socialist Group	81 Yes
12 French	17 Female	27 Christian Democratic Conservative Group	5 No
9 Swedish		5 Liberal/Reform Group	
6 Irish		13 Others	
2 Spanish			

*At the time of interview or when leaving the parliament.

The survey was administered in September 2000; response rates by nation were as detailed in Table A.2.

Further details about the survey, the complete data-set and an English version of the entire questionnaire used are publicly available from the website of the European Parliament Research Group: http://www.lse.ac.uk/Depts/eprg/.

Roll-Call Voting Data

The roll-call voting data analysed in Chapter 6 cover all votes held in plenary sessions of the EP (both in Brussels and Strasbourg) during the first six months of the 1999–2004 EP. The 241 votes covered by the data-set cover the range of legislative and non-legislative votes, with legislative votes taken under the consultation, co-decision and assent procedures and at varying stages of those procedures. The data was gathered as part of a joint research project by Professor Simon Hix, Dr Abdul Noury, and Dr Gerard

TABLE A.2

	Respondents	MEPs	Response rate (%)
Austria	2	21	9.5
Belgium	6	25	24.0
Denmark	7	16	43.8
Finland	7	16	43.8
France	22	87	25.3
Germany	27	99	27.3
Greece	8	25	32.0
Ireland	4	15	26.7
Italy	23	87	26.4
Luxembourg	5	6	83.3
Netherlands	15	31	48.4
Portugal	11	25	44.0
Spain	17	64	26.6
Sweden	10	22	45.5
UK	35	87	40.2
Total	199	626	31.8

Roland, and is publicly available from the website of the European Parliament Research Group: *http://www.lse.ac.uk/Depts/eprg/*.

References

Abeles, M. (1992), *La vie quotidienne au Parlement europeen*, Paris: Hachette.

Abramson, P. (1992), 'Of Time and Partisan Instability in Britain', *British Journal of Political Science*, 22(3): 381–95.

Alger, C. (1963), 'United Nations Participation as a Learning Experience', *Public Opinion Quarterly*, 27(3): 411–26.

Armstrong, K. and Bulmer, S. (1998), *The Governance of the Single European Market*, Manchester: Manchester University Press.

Arnold, L. (1998), 'Legislative Activity and Effectiveness in the US Senate: Reaping the Rewards of Seniority', Paper presented at the 1998 Annual Meeting of the Midwest Political Science Association, Chicago.

Aspinwall, M. and Schneider, G. (2000), 'Same Menu, Separate Tables: The Institutionalist Turn in Political Science and the Study of European Integration', *European Journal of Political Research*, 38(1): 1–36.

Asher, H. (1973), 'The Learning of Legislative Norms', *American Political Science Review*, 67(2): 499–513.

Bailer, S. and Schneider, G. (2000), 'The Power of Legislative Hot Air: Informal Rules and the Enlargement Debate in the European Parliament', *Journal of Legislative Studies*, 6(2): 19–44.

Bell, C. and Price, C. (1975), *The First Term: A Study in Legislative Socialization*, Beverly Hills, CA: Sage.

Bellier, I. (1997), 'The Commission as an Actor: an Anthropologist's View', in H. Wallace and A. Young (eds), *Participation and Policy-Making in the European Union*, Oxford: Clarendon Press.

Berger, P. and Luckmann, T. (1967), *The Social Construction of Reality: A Treatise in the Sociology of Knowledge*, London: Penguin.

Bonham, G. (1970), 'Participation in Regional Parliamentary Assemblies: Effects on Attitudes of Scandinavian Parliamentarians', *Journal of Common Market Studies*, 8(4): 325–36.

Bowler, S. and Farrell, D. (1995), 'The Organization of the European Parliament: Committees, Specialization and Co-ordination', *British Journal of Political Science*, 25(2) 219–43.

—— —— (1999), 'Parties and Party Discipline within the European Parliament: a Norms-Based Approach', in S. Bowler, D. Farrell and R. Katz (eds), *Party Discipline and Parliamentary Government*, Columbus: Ohio State University Press.

Burbank, M. (1997), 'Explaining Contextual Effects on Vote Choice', *Political Behavior*, 19(2) 113–32.

Brzinski, J., Gunning, H., Haspel, M., and Saunders, K. (1998), 'Understanding Defection in the European Parliament', Paper presented to the Annual Meeting of the American Political Science Association, Boston.

Boyce, B. (1995), 'The June 1994 Elections and the Politics of the European parliament', *Parliamentary Affairs*, 48(1): 141–56.

Bystydzienski, J. (1992), *Women Transforming Politics: Worldwide Strategies for Empowerment*, Bloomington, IND: Indiana University Press.

Carruba, C. (2001), 'The Electoral Connection in European Union Politics', *Journal of Politics*, 63(1): 141–58.

Checkel, J. (2001a), 'Why Comply? Social Learning and European Identity Change', *International Organization*, 55(3): 553–88.

—— (2001b), 'Forum: A Constructivist Research Program in EU Studies?', *European Union Politics*, 2(2): 219–26.

—— (2003), ' "Going Native" in Europe? Theorizing Social Interaction in European Institutions', *Comparative Political Studies*, 36(1/2): 209–31.

Chong, D. (1999), *Rational Lives: Norms and Values in Politics and Society*, Chicago: University of Chicago Press.

Christiansen, T., Jorgensen, K-E., and Wiener, A. (1999), 'The Social Construction of Europe', *Journal of European Public Policy*, 6(4): 528–44.

Cini, M. (1996), *The European Commission: Leadership, Organization and Culture in the EU Administration*, Manchester: Manchester University Press.

Clark, H. and Price, R. (1977), 'A note on the pre-nomination role socialization of freshmen members of Parliament', *Canadian Journal of Political Science*, 10(2): 319–406.

Converse, P. (1969), 'Of Time and Partisan Stability', *Comparative Political Studies*, 2(1): 139–71.

Corbett, R. (1996), 'Governance and Institutional Developments', *Journal of Common Market Studies*, 34(1): 29–42.

—— (1998), *The European Parliament's Role in Closer EU Integration*, Basingstoke, Macmillan.

—— (1999), 'The European Parliament and the Idea of European Representative Government', in J. Pinder (ed.), *Foundations of Democracy in the European Union: From the Genesis of Parliamentary Democracy to the European Parliament*, Basingstoke: Macmillan.

Corbett, R., Jacobs, F., and Shackleton, M. (1995), *The European Parliament*, 3rd edn, London: Cartermill.

——— , ——— , ——— (2000), *The European Parliament*, 4th edn, London: John Harper.

Cotta, M. (1984), 'Direct Elections of the European Parliament: A Supranational Political Elite in the Making?', in K. Reif (ed.), *European Elections 1979/81 and 1984: Conclusions and Perspectives from Empirical Research*, Berlin: Quorum.

Cram, L., Dinan, D. and Nugent, N. (1999), 'Reconciling Theory and Practice', in L. Cram, D. Dinan and N. Nugent (eds), *Developments in the European Union*, Basingstoke: Macmillan.

Deutsch, K. (1966), *Nationalism and Social Communication : an Inquiry into the Foundation of Nationality*, 2nd edn, Cambridge: MIT Press.

Dinan, D. (1999), *Ever Closer Union: An Introduction to European Integration*, 2nd edn, London: Macmillan.

Duff, A. (1994), 'Building a Parliamentary Europe', *Government and Opposition*, 29(1): 147–65.

Dunleavy, P. (1979), 'The urban basis of political alignment: Social class, property ownership and state intervention in consumption processes', *British Journal of Political Science*, 9(4): 409–43.

Dunphy, R. (1996), 'Conservative and Christian Democrat Debates on Europe', in P. Murray and P. Rich (eds), *Visions of European Unity*, Boulder, CO: Westview Press.

Eagly, A. and Chaiken, S. (1998), 'Attitude structure and function', in D. T. Gilbert, S. T. Fiske, and G. Lindzey (eds), *The Handbook of Social Psychology*, 4th edn, New York: McGraw-Hill.

van der Eijk, C. and Franklin, M. (eds) (1996), *Choosing Europe? The European Electorate and National Politics in the Face of Union*, Ann Arbor, MI: University of Michigan Press.

Faas, T. (2002), 'Why do MEPs Defect? National, Institutional and Party Group Pressures on MEPs and Their Consequences for Party Group Cohesion in the EP', paper presented to the Joint Sessions of the European Consortium for Political research, Turin.

Falcione, R. and Wilson, C. (1988), 'Socialization Processes in Organizations', in G. Goldhuber et al., (eds), *Handbook of Organizational Communication*, New Jersey: Ablex.

Farrell, D. and Scully, R. (2003), 'Electoral Reform and the British MEP', *Journal of Legislative Studies*, 9(1): 14–36.

Featherstone, K. (1979), 'Labour in Europe: The Work of a National Party Delegation to The European Parliament', in V. Herman and R. Van Schendelen (eds), *The European Parliament and the National Parliaments*, Farnborough: Saxon House.

Feld, W. and Wildgen, J. (1975), 'Electoral Ambitions and European Integration', *International Organization*, 29(2): 447–68.

Feldman, D. (1976), 'A Contingency Theory of Socialisation', *Administrative Science Quarterly*, 21: 433–50.

Feldman, D. (1981), 'The Multiple Socialization of Organizational Members', *Academy of Management Review*, 6(2): 309–18.

Fenno, R. (1962), 'The House Appropriations Committee as a Political System', *American Political Science Review*, 56(2): 310–24.

—— (1973), *Congressmen in Committees*, Boston, MA: Little, Brown.

—— (1978), *Home Style: House Members in Their Districts*, Boston, MA: Little, Brown.

Fiellen, A. (1962), 'The Functions of Informal Groups in Legislative Institutions', *Journal of Politics*, 24(1): 72–91.

Franklin, M. and Scarrow, S. (1999), 'Making Europeans? The Socialising Power of the European Parliament', in R. Katz and B. Wessels (eds), *The European Parliament, the National Parliaments, and European Integration*, Oxford: Oxford University Press.

Friedman, J. (ed.) (1996), *The Rational Choice Controversy: Economic Models of Politics Reconsidered*, New Haven, CT: Yale University Press.

Gareau, F. (1978), 'Congressional Representatives to the UN General Assembly: "Corruption" by Foreign Gentry', *Orbis*, 21(3): 701–24.

Garrett, G. and Tsebelis, G. (1996), 'An Institutional Critique of Intergovernmentalism', *International Organization*, 50(2): 269–99.

Garrett, G. and Tsebelis, G. (2000), 'Legislative Politics in the European Union', *European Union Politics*, 1(1): 9–36.

Glarbo, K. (1999), 'Wide-awake diplomacy: Reconstructing the Common Foreign and Security Policy of The European Union', *Journal of European Public Policy*, 6(4): 634–51.

Green, D. and Shapiro, I. (1994), *Pathologies of Rational Choice Theory*, New Haven, CT: Yale University Press.

Gross, P. and Levitt, N. (1998), *Higher Superstition: The Academic Left and its Quarrels with Science*, 2nd edn, London: Johns Hopkins University Press.

Haas, E. (1968), *The Uniting of Europe: Political, Social and Economic Forces* 2nd edn, Stanford: Stanford University Press.

—— (1971), 'The Study of Regional Integration: Reflections on the Joy and Anguish of Pretheorizing', in L. Lindberg and S. Scheingold (eds), *Euro-*

pean Integration: Theory and Research, Cambridge, MA: Harvard University Press.

Hagger, M. and Wing, M. (1979), 'Legislative Roles and Clientele Orientations in the European Parliament', *Legislative Studies Quarterly*, 4(2): 165–96.

Hagle, T. (1993), ' "Freshman Effects" for Supreme Court Justices', *American Journal of Political Science*, 37(4): 1142–57.

Hall, R. (1987), 'Participation and Purpose in Committee Decision-Making', *American Political Science Review*, 81(1): 105–27.

Hayes-Renshaw, F. and Wallace, H. (1997), *The Council of Ministers*, Basingstoke: Macmillan.

Hrbek, R. (1990), 'The Impact of EC Membership on Political Parties and Pressure Groups', in C. Schweitzer and D. Karsten (eds), *The Federal Republic of Germany and EC Membership Evaluated*, London: Pinter.

Hewstone, M. (1985), *Understanding Attitudes to the European Community: A Social-Psychological Study in Four Member States*, Cambridge: Cambridge University Press.

Hix, S. (2002a), 'Parliamentary Behavior with Two Principals: Preferences, Parties, and Voting in the European Parliament', *American Journal of Political Science*, 46(3): 688–98.

—— (2002b), 'Constitutional Agenda-Setting Through Discretion in Rule Interpretation: Why the European Parliament Won at Amsterdam', *British Journal of Political Science*, 32(2) 259–80.

—— (2005), *The Political System of the European Union, 2nd edn*, Basingstoke: Palgrave Macmillan.

—— (2003), 'How Electoral Institutions Shape Legislative Behaviour: Explaining Voting Defection in the European Parliament', *European Parliament Research Group Working Paper 10*.

Hix, S. and Lord, C. (1996), 'The Making of a President: the European Parliament and the Confirmation of Jacques Santer as President of the Commission', *Government and Opposition* 31(1): 62–76.

—— —— (1997), *Political Parties and the European Union,Basingstoke*: Macmillan.

Hix, S. Kreppel, A., and Noury, A. (2003), 'The Party System in the European Parliament: Collusive or Competitive', *Journal of Common Market Studies*, 41(2): 309–31.

Hooghe, L. (1999a), 'Images of Europe: Orientations to European Integration among Senior Officials of the Commission', *British Journal of Political Science*, 29(2): 345–67.

Hooghe, L. (1999b), 'Supranational Activists or Intergovernmental Agents? Explaining the Orientations of Senior Commission Officials Toward European Integration', *Comparative Political Studies*, 32(4): 435–63.

Hooghe, L. (2001), *The European Commission and the Integration of Europe: Images of Governance*, Cambridge: Cambridge University Press.

Hopf, T. (2002), *Social Construction of International Politics: Identities and Foreign Policies, Moscow 1955 & 1999*, Ithaca: Cornell University Press.

Huber, J. and Inglehart, R., (1995), 'Expert Interpretations of Party Space and Party Locations in 42 Societies', *Party Politics*, 1(1): 73–111.

Jachtenfuchs, M., Diez, T., and Jung, S., (1998), 'Which Europe? Conflicting Models of a Legitimate European Political Order', *European Journal of International Relations*, 4(4): 409–45.

Jackson, C. (1993), 'The First British MEPs: Styles and Strategies', *Contemporary European History*, 2(2): 169–95.

Jacobson, H. (1967), 'Deriving Data from Delegates to International Assemblies', *International Organization*, 21(3): 592–613.

Jepperson, R. (1991), 'Institutions, Institutional Effects, and Institutionalism', in W. Powell and P. DiMaggio (eds), *The New Institutionalism in Organizational Analysis*, Chicago: University of Chicago Press.

Johanssen, K-M. (1995), 'Party Group Dynamics in the European Parliament', Unpublished Mimeo, University of Lund.

Johnston, A. (2001), 'Treating International Institutions as Social Environments', *International Studies Quarterly*, 45(4): 487–515.

Karns, D. (1977), 'The Effect of Interparliamentary Meetings on the Foreign Policy Attitudes of United States Congressmen', *International Organization*, 31(3): 497–513.

Katz, R. (1999), 'Representation, the locus of democratic legitimation, and the role of the national parliament in the European Union', in R. Katz and B. Wessels (eds), *The European Parliament, the National Parliaments, and European Integration*, Oxford: Oxford University Press.

—— and Wessels, B. (1999), *The European Parliament, the National Parliaments, and European Integration*, Oxford: Oxford University Press.

Kelman, H. (1966), 'Social-Psychological Approaches to the Study of International Relations: the Questions of Relevance', in H. Kelman (ed.), *International Behavior*, New York: Holt, Reinhart and Winston, pp. 565–607.

Kerr, H. (1973), 'Changing Attitudes Through International Participation: European Parliamentarians and Integration', *International Organization*, 27(1): 45–83.

King, G., Keohane, R. and Verba, S. (1994), *Designing Social Inquiry: Scientific Inference in Qualitative Research*, Princeton: Princeton University Press.

Kirchner, E. (1984), 'The European Parliament: Performance and Prospects', Aldershot, UK: Dartmouth.

Kornberg and Thomas, N. (1965), 'The Political Socialization of National Elites in the United States and Canada', *Journal of Politics*, 21 (4): 761–75

Kreppel, A. (1999), 'What Affects the European Parliament's Legislative Influence? An Analysis of the Success of EP Amendments', *Journal of Common Market Studies*, 37: 521–37.

—— (2002), *The European Parliament and Supranational Party System: A Study in Institutional Development*, Cambridge: Cambridge University Press.

—— and Tsebelis, G. (1999), 'Coalition Formation in the European Parliament', *Comparative Political Studies*, 32(4): 933–66.

Laver, M. and Hunt, B. (1992), *Policy and Party Competition*, New York: Routledge.

Lindberg, L. (1963), *The Political Dynamics of European Integration*, Oxford: Oxford University Press.

—— (1965), 'Decision Making and Integration in the European Community', *International Organization*, 19 (1): 56–80.

—— (1966), 'The Role of the European Parliament in an Emerging European Community', in E. Frank (ed.), *Lawyers in a Changing World*, Englewood Cliffs, NJ: Prentice-Hall.

Lewis, J. (1998), 'The the "Hard Bargaining" Image of the Council Misleading? The Committee of Permanent Representatives and the Local Elections Directive', *Journal of Common Market Studies*, 36(4): 479–504.

Louis, M. (1980), 'Surprise and Sense-Making: What Newcomers Experience in Entering Unfamiliar Settings', *Administrative Science Quarterly*, 25 (2): 226–51.

Lubbers, M. (2000), 'Expert Judgement Survey of Western European Political Parties 2000' [machine readable data set] Nijmegen, the Netherlands: NWO, Department of Sociology, University of Nijmegen.

McGilvray, J. (1999), *Chomsky: Language, Mind and Politics*, Cambridge: Polity Press.

van Maanen, J. and Schein, E. (1979), 'Toward a Theory of Organizational Socialization', *Research in Organizational Behavior*, 1 (2): 209–64.

March, J. and Olsen, J. (1989), *Rediscovering Institutions: The Organizational Basis of Politics*, New York: Free Press.

March, J. and Olsen, J. (1998), 'The Institutional Dynamics of International Political Orders', *International Organization*, 52 (4): 943–69.

Marquand, D. (1979), *Parliament for Europe*, London: Jonathon Cape.

Marsh, M. and Wessels, B. (1997), 'Territorial Representation', *European Journal of Political Research*, 32 (2): 227–41.

Matthews, D. (1960), *US Senators and their World*, New York: Vintage Books.

Mayhew, D. (1974), *Congress: The Electoral Connection*, New Haven, CT: Yale University Press.

Mezey, M. (1993), 'Legislatures: Individual Purpose and Institutional Performance', in A. Finifter (ed.), *Political Science: The State of the Discipline II*, Washington D.C.: American Political Science Association.

Mitrany, D. (1946), *A Working Peace System: An Argument for the Functional Developmental of International Organization*, 4th edn, London: National Peace Council.

Moravcsik, A. (1991), 'Negotiating the Single European Act: National Interests and Conventional Statecraft in the European Community', *International Organization*, 45(1): 19–56.

—— (1993), 'Preferences and Power in the European Community: a Liberal Intergovernmentalist Approach', *Journal of Common Market Studies*, 31(4): 473–524.

—— (1994), 'Why the European Community Strengthens the State: Domestic Politics and International Cooperation', Center for European Studies Working Paper 52, Harvard University.

—— (1998), *The Choice for Europe: Social Purpose and State Power From Messina to Maastricht*, London: UCL Press.

—— (1999), 'A New Statecraft? Supranational Entrepreneurs and International Cooperation', *International Organization*, 53 (2): 267–306.

—— (2001), 'Forum: A Constructivist Research Program in EU Studies?', *European Union Politics*, 2 (2): 226–40.

Moser, P. (1996), 'The European Parliament as a Conditional Agenda Setter: What are the Conditions?', *American Political Science Review*, 90 (4): 834–38.

Mughan, A., Box-Steffensmeier, J., and Scully, R. (1997), 'Mapping Legislative Socialization', *European Journal of Political Research*, 33 (1): 93–106.

Neunreither, Karlheinz (2000), 'Political Representation in the European Union: A Common Whole, Various Wholes, or Just a Hole?', in K. Neunreither and A. Weiner (eds), *European Integration After Amsterdam: Institutional Dynamics and Prospects for Democracy*, Oxford: Oxford University Press.

Norris, P. and Lovenduski, J. (1996), *Women in Politics*, Oxford: Oxford University Press.

Nugent, N. (1999), *The Government and Politics of the European Union*, 4th edn, London: Macmillan.

O'Neill, M. (1996), *The Politics of European Integration: A Reader*, London: Routledge.

Ostroff, C. and Kozlowski, S. (1992), 'Organizational Socialization as a Learning Process: the Role of Information Acquisition', *Personnel Psychology*, 45 (x): 849–74.

Ovey, J. D. (2000), 'Determining MEP Autonomy: Positive and Negative "detachment" and the Structuring of Relations Between National Parties and MEPs', unpublished paper, University of Osnabruck.

Pappamikail, P. (1998), 'Britain Viewed from Europe', in D. Baker and D. Seawright (eds) *Britain For and Against Europe*, Oxford: Clarendon Press.

Peck, R. (1979), 'Socialization of Permanent Representatives in the United Nations: Some Evidence', *International Organization*, 33 (3): 365–90.

Pendergast, W. (1976), 'Roles and Attitudes of French and Italian Delegates to the European Community', *International Organization*, 30 (4): 669–77.

Pennings, P., Keman, H. and Kleinnijenhuis, J. (1999), *Doing Research in Political Science: an introduction to comparative methods and statistics*, London: Sage.

Peters, B. (1999), *Institutional Theory in Political Science: the 'New Institutionalism'*, London: Pinter.

Peterson, J. (1997), 'States, Societies and the European Union', *West European Politics*, 20 (4): 1–23.

Pinker, S. (1995), *The Language Instinct: The New Science of Language and Mind*, London: Penguin.

Pollack, M. (1998), 'Constructivism, Social Psychology and Elite Attitude Change: Lessons from an Exhausted Research Program', Paper presented to the Conference of Europeanists, Baltimore.

—— (2001), 'International Relations Theory and European Integration', *Journal of Common Market Studies*, 39 (2): 221–44.

Powell, W. and DiMaggio, P. (1991), 'Introduction', in W. Powell and P. DiMaggio (eds), *The New Institutionalism in Organizational Analysis*, Chicago: University of Chicago Press.

Prost, A. and Rosenveig, C. (1977), 'Measurement of Attitude Changes Among the Members of the French Chamber of Deputies, 1882–84' in

W. O. Aydelotte (ed.), *The History of Parliamentary Behavior*, Princeton, NJ: Princeton University Press.

Putnam, R. (1993), *Making Democracy Work: Civic Traditions in Modern Italy*, Princeton: NJ: Princeton University Press.

Raunio, T. (1997), *The European Perspective: Transnational Party Groups in the 1989–1994 European Parliament*, Aldershot: Ashgate.

—— (2000), 'Losing Independence or Finally Gaining Recognition? Contacts Between MEPs and National Parties', *Party Politics*, 6 (2): 211–24.

Ray, L. (1999), 'Measuring Party Orientations Towards European Integration: Results from an Expert Survey', *European Journal for Political Research*, 36(2): 283–306.

Rich, P. (1996), 'Visionary Ideals of European Unity After World War I', in P. Murray and P. Rich (eds), *Visions of European Unity*, Boulder, CO: Westview.

Riggs, R. (1977), 'One Small Step for Functionalism', *International Organization*, 31 (3): 515–39.

Riggs, R. and Mykleton, I. (1979), *Beyond Functionalism: Attitudes Toward International Organization in Norway and the United States*, Minneapolis, MN: University of Minnesota Press.

Risse, T. (2000), 'Let's Argue! Communicative Action in World Politics', *International Organization*, 54 (1): 1–39.

—— (2004), 'Social Constructivism and European Integration', in A. Wiener and T. Diex (eds), *European Integration Theory*, Oxford: Oxford University Press.

Rittberger, B. (2000), 'Impatient Legislators and New Issue-Dimensions: A Critique of the Garrett-Tsebelis "Standard Version" of Legislative Politics', *Journal of European Public Policy*, 7 (4): 554–75.

—— (2003), 'The Creation and Empowerment of the European Parliament', *Journal of Common Market Studies*, 41 (2): 203–26.

Rosamund, B. (2000), *Theories of European Integration*, Basingstoke: Macmillan.

Sandholtz, W. and Stone Sweet, A. (eds) (1998), *European Integration and Supranational Governance*, Oxford: Oxford University Press.

Scarrow, S. (1997), 'Political Career Paths and the European Parliament', *Legislative Studies Quarterly*, 22 (2): 253–63.

Schmitter, P. (1971), 'A revised Theory of European Integration', in L. Lindberg and S. Scheingold (eds), *European Integration: Theory and Research*, Cambridge, MA: Harvard University Press.

Scully, R. (1997a), 'The European Parliament and the Co-Decision Procedure: A Re-Assessment', *Journal of Legislative Studies*, 3 (3): 58–73.

—— (1997b), 'The European Parliament and Co-Decision: A Rejoinder to Tsebelis and Garrett', *Journal of Legislative Studies*, 3 (1): 93–103.

—— (1998), 'MEPs and the Building of a "Parliamentary Europe" ', *Journal of Legislative Studies*, 4 (3): 92–108.

—— (2002), 'Going Native? Institutional and Partisan Loyalty in the European Parliament', in B. Steunenberg and J. Thomassen (eds), *The European Parliament: Moving Towards Democracy in the EU*, London: Rowman & Littlefield.

—— (2003), 'The European Parliament', in M. Cini (ed.), *European Union Politics*, Oxford: Oxford University Press.

—— Hix, S. and Raunio, T. (1999), 'An Institutional Theory of the Behaviour of MEPs', Paper presented to the biennial Conference of the European Community Studies Association, Pittsburgh.

—— Rauio, T., and Hix, S. (1999), 'Towards An Institutionalist Theory of Behaviour in the European Parliament', Paper presented to the Biennial Conference of the European Community Studies Association, Pittsburgh.

Searing, D. (1986), 'A Theory of Political Socialization: Institutional Support and Deradicalization in Britain', *British Journal of Political Science*, 16 (3): 341–76.

—— (1994), *Westminster's World: Understanding Political Roles*, Cambridge, MA: Harvard University Press.

Shackleton, Michael (2000), 'The Politics of Codecision', *Journal of Common Market Studies*, 38: 325–42.

Shepherd, M. (1996), 'Term Limits: Evidence of Careerism and Socialization in the US House of Representatives', *Journal of Legislative Studies*, 2 (2): 245–66.

Skinner, B. (1957), *Verbal Behaviour*, Eaglewood Cliffs, NJ: Prentice-Hall.

Smith, K. (1973), 'The European Economic Community and National Civil Servants of the Member States: A Comment', *International Organization*, 27 (4): 563–68.

Spinelli, A. (1996), *The Eurocrats: Conflict and Crisis in the European Community*, Baltimore, MD: Johns Hopkins Press.

Stone Sweet, A. and Sandholtz, W. (1997), 'European Integration and Supranational Governance', *Journal of European Public Policy*, 4 (3): 297–317.

Strom, K. (1990), 'A Behavioural Theory of Competitive Political Parties', *American Journal of Political Science*, 34 (2): 565–98.

Taggart, P. (1998), 'A Touchstone of Dissent: Euroscepticism in Contemporary Western European Party Systems', *European Journal of Political Research*, 33(2): 363–88.

—— and Szczerbiak, A. (2004), *Opposing Europe? The Comparative Party Politics of Euroscepticism*, Volume 1: *Case Studies and Country Surveys*, Oxford: Oxford University Press.

Thelen, K. and Steinmo, S. (1992), 'Historical Institutionalism in Comparative Politics', in S. Steinmo, K. Thelen and F. Longstreth (eds), *Structuring Politics: Historical Institutionalism in Comparative Politics*, Cambridge: Cambridge University Press.

Trondal, J. (2001), 'Is there any social constructivist-institutionalist divide? Unpacking social mechanisms affecting representational roles among EU decision-makers', *Journal of European Public Policy*, 8(1): 1–23.

Tsebelis, G. (2002), *Veto Players: How Political Institutions Work*, Princeton: Princeton University Press.

—— and Garrett, G. (1997), 'Agenda Setting, Vetoes and the European Union's Co-decision Procedure', *Journal of Legislative Studies*, 3 (3): 74–92.

—— —— (2001), 'The Institutional Foundations of Intergovernmentalism and Supranationalism in the European Union', *International Organization*, 55 (2): 357–90.

—— ., Christian, B. J., Kalandrakis, A. and Kreppel, A. (2001), 'Legislative Procedures in the European Union: An Empirical Analysis', *British Journal of Political Science*, 31: 573–99.

Wendt, A. (1992), 'Anarchy Is What States Make of It', *International Organization*, 46 (2): 391–425.

Westlake, M. (1994), *Britain's Emerging Euro-Elite? The British in the Directly Elected European Parliament, 1979–1992*, Aldershot, UK: Dartmouth.

Whitaker, R. (2001), 'Party Control in a Committee-Based Legislature? The Case of the European Parliament', *Journal of Legislative Studies*, 7(4): 63–88.

Wind, M. (1997), 'Rediscovering Institutions: a reflectivist critique of rational institutionalism', in K.-E. Jorgensen (ed.), *Reflective Approaches to European Governance*, Basingstoke: Macmillan.

Zimbardo, P. and Leippe, M. (1991), *The Psychology of Attitude Change and Social Influence*, New York: McGraw-Hill.

Index